Sophocles lived betw   plays are
Ajax (c. 442 BC), *Antig   , Oedipus the King* (c. 429 BC),
Philoctetes (c. 409 BC), *Oedipus at Kolonos* (406 BC),
Women of Trachis (date unknown) and *Electra* (date unknown).

TIMBERLAKE WERTENBAKER

Timberlake Wertenbaker's plays include *New Anatomies,*
Abel's Sister, The Grace of Mary Traverse, Our Country's
*Good, The Love of the Nightingale, Three Bi   *
Field, The Break of Day, After Darwin, The Ash Girl and *Credible*
Witness. She translates from French, Italian and Greek, and
her many translations and adaptations include *Successful*
Strategies, False Admissions and *La Dispute* by Marivaux,
Leocadia by Anouilh, *Pelleas and Melisande* by Maeterlinck,
Mephisto by Arianne Mnouchkine, *The Way You Want Me* by
Pirandello and *Hebuka* by Euripides. The three plays in this
volume were presented by the Royal Shakespeare Company
in 1991 at *The Thebans*.

SOPHOCLES

Oedipus Tyrannos
Oedipus at Kolonos
Antigone

translated by
Timberlake Wertenbaker

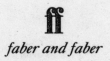

faber and faber

First published in 1992 as *The Thebans*
by Faber and Faber Limited
3 Queen Square London WCIN 3AU
Reprinted with corrections 1994
This edition first published in 1997

Typeset by Parker Typesetting Service, Leicester
Printed in England by Mackays of Chatham plc, Chatham, Kent

A CIP record for this book is available from the British Library

ISBN 978-0-571-19535-0
ISBN 0-571-19535-0

4 6 8 10 9 7 5

For J.

CONTENTS

The Thebans was first performed at the Swan Theatre, Stratford-upon-Avon, on 25 and 26 October 1991. The cast was as follows:

Oedipus Tyrannos

OEDIPUS	Gerard Murphy
A PRIEST OF ZEUS	Christopher Saul
KREON	John Shrapnel
TEIRESIAS	Clifford Rose
HIS BOY	Edmund Kinglsey/
	Jonathan Woolf
JOKASTA	Linda Marlowe
A MESSENGER FROM	
KORINTH	Denys Hawthorne
A HERDSMAN	Richard Moore
A MESSENGER FROM	
THE PALACE	Valerie Sarruf
CHORUS	
Josette Bushell-Mingo	Richard Moore
Virginia Denham	Siân Radinger
Michael Gould	Valerie Sarruf
Ian Hughes	Christopher Saul
Paul Kiernan	Angus Wright

Oedipus at Kolonos

OEDIPUS	Gerard Murphy
ANTIGONE	Joanne Pearce
A LOCAL MAN	Denys Hawthorne
ISMENE	Linda Bassett
THESEUS	Philip Voss
KREON	John Shrapnel
POLYNEIKES	Rob Edwards
A MESSENGER	Clifford Rose

CHORUS

Josette Bushell-Mingo	Richard Moore
Virginia Denham	Siân Radinger
Michael Gould	Valerie Sarruf
Ian Hughes	Christopher Saul
Paul Kiernan	Angus Wright

Antigone

ANTIGONE	Joanne Pearce
ISMENE	Linda Bassett
KREON	John Shrapnel
SOLDIER	Richard Moore
HAIMON	Paul Kiernan
TEIRESIAS	Clifford Rose
HIS BOY	Edmund Kingsley/ Jonathan Woolf
A MESSENGER	Ian Hughes
EURYDIKE	Valerie Sarruf

CHORUS

Josette Bushell-Mingo	Gerard Murphy
Virginia Denham	Siân Radinger
Rob Edwards	Christopher Saul
Michael Gould	Angus Wright

Director	Adrian Noble
Designer	Ultz
Lighting	Alan Burrell
Music	Ilona Sekacz
Movement Director	Sue Lefton

The author would like to thank Neil Croally and Margaret Williamson for their help with Sophocles' text.

CHARACTERS

OEDIPUS

JOKASTA, wife of Oedipus, widow of Laios

KREON, brother of Jokasta, uncle of Antigone and Ismene

ANTIGONE, daughter of Oedipus and Jokasta

ISMENE, daughter of Oedipus and Jokasta

POLYNEIKES, son of Oedipus and Jokasta

EURIDIKE, wife of Kreon

HAIMON, son of Kreon and Euridike

TEIRESIAS, a blind prophet

A BOY, guide to Teiresias

A PRIEST OF ZEUS

A HERDSMAN

A LOCAL MAN

THESEUS, King of Athens

A SOLDIER

MESSENGERS

CHORUS

OEDIPUS TYRANNOS

PROLOGUE

Thebes.

OEDIPUS: Children of Thebes, why are you sitting here?
The city overflows: incense, prayers for the sick, moans –
I didn't want to hear the second-hand reports of some
messenger, so I have come myself, the renowned Oedipus.
Old man, you look like a fit spokesman for these people. Tell
me, why have you come? Is it fear? Something you want? You
know I will do what I can. I would be shorn of all compassion
if I didn't pity you, now, as you sit here.

PRIEST: Oedipus, you are the ruler of our land.
Look at us: fledgelings over here; over there, bodies bent with
age; myself, a priest of Zeus: here. And there, the best of our
youth. Others have gone to the two temples of Athene to try
and find some guidance – a prophecy – in the ashes of the
altars. Our city tosses in a storm, plunging into the troughs of
bloody waves. Desolation everywhere. Wasted cattle grazing
wasting fields, ravaged women bearing shreds of wasted
children. This feverish god presses down his hateful plague
on the inhabitants of Thebes and death reaps the laments.
It is not that we think of you as a god. But you are a man with
much experience. And in touch with spiritual matters. It was
you who came to Thebes and rid us of that relentless tax, the
cruel Songstress.
A god must have helped you then to bring back order into
our lives. And now, all-powerful Oedipus, you must help us
again, whether you have to seek divine inspiration or the help
of mere men. I know that a man who has experienced much
in the past can give effective advice about the future. You are
celebrated for your former actions. Don't let yourself be
remembered as the one who saved the city only to destroy it.
Bring us security, as before, when you appeared to us like the
promise of good fortune. You want to be master of this land –
what reward in ruling over a deserted city? No ship, no

3

battlement is worth much once emptied of the living.

OEDIPUS: Children, I know all this. I know of your pain, which is great, but not as great as mine. Each of you feels only for himself. I feel for the city, for myself, and for all of you. I have not slept, I have been weeping, explored endless avenues of thought. I came up with one possible remedy, which I immediately put into action.

I've sent my brother-in-law Kreon to the Oracle of Apollo to discover what I might do or say to save this city. He left some time ago. Too long ago. This worries me.

When he comes back, I'll do what I must. Only a bad man would ignore what the God says.

PRIEST: You've spoken well. Some people have just seen Kreon. They're signalling to me.

OEDIPUS: Apollo, let his untroubled countenance signify untroubled fortunes.

PRIEST: He seems to bring good news. He's crowned with laurels.

OEDIPUS: We'll know soon enough.

(KREON and OEDIPUS greet each other.)

Kreon.

Kinsman.

What has the God said?

KREON: Good things. Even the greatest troubles, once put right, end well.

OEDIPUS: What are you saying? Your words don't alarm, don't reassure.

KREON: If you want these people to hear, I'll speak. Otherwise, we can go inside.

OEDIPUS: Speak in front of everyone. I bear more pain for these people than for my own soul.

KREON: This is what I heard from the God.

Apollo urged us clearly to drive out the pollution – a defilement, nurtured in this land. Not to let this deadly thing grow, until the damage becomes irreparable, incurable.

OEDIPUS: How do we purify our land? What's causing this?

KREON: By banishment; or spilling blood for blood. Blood that is wrecking our city.

4

OEDIPUS: Who is the man who must suffer such a fate?

KREON: Before you governed this city, Laios was our ruler.

OEDIPUS: I heard of him but never saw him.

KREON: We are ordered to punish his murderers, whoever they may be.

OEDIPUS: Where on earth are they? How can we find traces of this hidden crime?

KREON: He said in this land. What is sought is found, what is kept dark remains hidden.

OEDIPUS: Was Laios at home, in the country, abroad when he died?

KREON: He was on his way to the Oracle. He never returned.

OEDIPUS: Did no messenger come and report? Did none who travelled with him see anything?

KREON: All died, except for one. He fled, terrified, and assured us he had nothing to say. He was certain of only one thing.

OEDIPUS: What? We can hope to learn a lot from a small fact.

KREON: He spoke of several robbers falling on him; of the strength of many hands.

OEDIPUS: How could a robber be so bold unless he were paid and sent from here?

KREON: We thought of that, but with Laios murdered, we had no one to help us in the terrible troubles that followed.

OEDIPUS: What troubles could be so great they kept you from seeking the murderer of your king?

KREON: The Sphinx sang her riddles – she forced us to deal with the immediate and forget a murky past.

OEDIPUS: I will start again and make everything clear.
It was right of the God and proper of you to turn your attention to the matter of this dead man. And you will find in me an ally of this man and of the God. I will rid us of this abomination, not only on behalf of distant friends but for my own sake. Whoever killed that man could apply an equally fierce hand to my person. I must help Laios and myself at the same time. And now, children of Thebes, you can rise from these steps, take away your branches and let all of Thebes know that I mean to leave nothing untried. With the help of

5

the God, we will bring everything to light; or else we will fall.

PRIEST: Let us go. We have obtained what we sought from this man. And may Phoibus, having given his oracle, come to us, save us, and heal us.

FIRST CHORUS

CHORUS

Welcome voice of Zeus, come
to famous Thebes from
gold-rich Delphi. But for
what?

oh dios haduepes Phati

Fear: my heart beats,
shakes. This fear: torture.
Terror racks me.

ektetamai
ektetamai

Delian healer,
awe-cloaked.
Is this a new calamity,
unknown? Or the return,
seasonal, revolving, of
something past?

ieeieh
Dalie Paian

Tell me, deathless voice,
child of golden hope

eipe moi, oh chruseas
teknon Elpidos, ambrote
Phama

We call on you first,
daughter of Zeus, eternal
Athene.

ambrot'Athana

And then on your sister,
earth-encircling Artemis,
whose throne dominates our
marketplace.

gaiaochon t'adelphean
Artemin

And on Apollo, whose darts
no one escapes.
You can turn fate back –
away.
Come to me
if you ever drove suffering

kai Phoibon hekabolon

7

from our borders once
before, then come again
now.

elthete kai nun

I bear countless sorrows.
All my citizens ill. No
spear-like thought to cut
us free. Nothing grows in
the earth, nothing in the
wombs of women. Look: one
life after another flies off,
swifter than a bird.
Death speeds, with the
crackle of a forest fire.

oh popoi

The city dies again and
again. Offspring lie on the
ground spreading death. No
one pities their pain. No
one laments their end.
Wives, mothers, grey-
haired, come from all parts
to the steps of the altars,
crying out the bitterness
of pain.
Prayers for healing – cries
for the dead – mount in
unison.

From all this, golden
daughter of Zeus, friend,
defend us.
Give us strength.

oh chrusea thugater Dios

Let the plague-bearing God
Ares – appearing not in
the bronzed glitter of

8

war, but in a mantle of
screams – let him turn
back, away from our
borders, blown over the
Atlantic, or sent north to
the black shores of Thrace.

Whatever escapes
destruction at night
succumbs by day.
Zeus, master of lightning,   *oh Zeu pater*
of fire, smash this god of
plague with your thunder.

Apollo, god of light, defend   *Lukei anax*
us with your golden
arrows.
Artemis, defend us with the   *Artemidos aiglas*
hunting flares that sparkle
on your hills.

And Bakchos, companion of   *oinopa Bacchon ee-u-ion*
the Maenads, Bakchos of   *ee-u-ion*
the golden headband and
face flushed with wine,
defend us with the flame of
your torches –
You three gods,
come and defend us against   *ton apotimon en*
this ungoldly god.   *Theois Theon*

FIRST EPISODE

OEDIPUS: You pray and I can help you with your troubles if you
listen to what I have to say and make the effort to help
yourselves.

I speak as a stranger to this story, a stranger to these events.
Not able to track anything down without some sign.

But since I am now rated your countryman, I have this to say
to you, Thebans:

Whoever knows what man killed Laios, that man must reveal
himself to me. And if he is afraid, let him know that if he
denounces himself, and does not wait for another to point
him out, he will suffer nothing worse than to leave the land,
unharmed.

And if someone knows this murderer, whether he comes
from here or from abroad, let him speak. He will be paid,
favoured. I will do this out of gratitude.

But if you insist on keeping silent, fearing for a friend or for
yourselves, then I will do the following. Listen carefully:

Whoever this man is, I forbid anyone in this land, over which I
hold power and favour, I forbid anyone to receive him at
home, to give him water, to pray with him or to join him in
sacrifices to the gods. I order everyone to drive this man out,
for this man is the pollution, the blight in our midst – the
pollution the Pythian God has revealed to me.

I will be God's ally, and this murdered man's. And I pray that
the killer, whether he lives in secret or is known to many, I
pray this man's pitiful life collapses and crumbles in wretched
decay.

And I also pray that if this man should be sharing my house,
unknown to me, or if I should be harbouring him knowingly,
then I pray that the same wretchedness befall me as I have just
called down on these people.

And I am relying on you to help me achieve this end, for my
own sake, for the sake of the God and for the sake of this
land, which is dying, without fruit, abandoned by the God.

And I say that even if the God had not sent you this plague, it was still wrong of you to allow this defilement. Your own king, the best of men, was killed. You ought to have looked into it. But now, I hold this man's power, his bed, and the same woman who was his wife. And if he had not been unlucky in his hope of a family, we would have children in common. But fate cut that man down. And so I will fight for him, as if he were my own father. I will attain my end and catch the murderer amongst us.

And I pray that anyone who tries to hinder me be deprived of the fruit of the earth, of children, that his destiny be one of ruin, and worse.

And you Thebans, who approve of what I have said, may Justice be your ally and the gods your friends.

CHORUS: I will now speak under oath, lord. I did not kill him nor can I point to the killer. But since this request comes from Apollo, can he not tell us who did it?

OEDIPUS: No man can compel the gods against their will.

CHORUS: I could suggest the second-best thing.

OEDIPUS: Don't neglect even a third possibility.

CHORUS: There is Teiresias – he sees eye to eye with Apollo. He could clarify the matter.

OEDIPUS: I can tell you that I've neglected nothing and, at Kreon's suggestion, I've sent for him twice. His delay is odd.

CHORUS: Some old and muted rumours . . .

OEDIPUS: What? I'll examine all reports . . .

CHORUS: It was said he was killed by travellers.

OEDIPUS: Yes, but no one has seen the survivor.

CHORUS: When the murderer hears your curses, he'll flee in terror.

OEDIPUS: He will not be afraid of words who is not afraid to act.

CHORUS: The man who can convict him is being led this way. The man of truth. The divine prophet.

(TEIRESIAS enters.)

OEDIPUS: Teiresias, you can fathom many things, hidden, manifest, heavenly, earth-bound.

You do not see, but you know the affliction that wraps this city. And now, only you can protect us, only you can save us. We are instructed by the God to find the killers of Laios – you

II

have probably already heard this. Please withhold nothing: a message from the birds, another form of divination . . . And rescue yourself, me, and all of us from this terrible pollution. We depend on you. The man who applies all of his resources, all of his faculties to help others is a noble man indeed.

TEIRESIAS: *Feu, feu.*

To understand – and there is no good in understanding. I had known, I had let it go . . . I wouldn't have come here.

OEDIPUS: What's this? So despondent?

TEIRESIAS: Let me go home. You'll live out your life more easily; so will I.

OEDIPUS: It is not right or friendly to speak like this to a city which keeps you. You must not hold back.

TEIRESIAS: Your words are ill-judged. I don't want mine to be.

OEDIPUS: Don't, when you have knowledge from the gods, turn away from us. We all prostrate ourselves before you. We beg you.

TEIRESIAS: You all know nothing. I cannot reveal my troubles – yours.

OEDIPUS: What? You know something but won't speak. You're willing to betray us and ruin the city?

TEIRESIAS: I won't distress you or myself. Why do you tease these things in vain? Will you not listen to me?

OEDIPUS: Evil of evil men, you'd anger a rock. Won't you speak? Won't you come to the point?

TEIRESIAS: You complain of my temper. You don't see what you live with.

OEDIPUS: Who wouldn't be angered listening to you insult the city.

TEIRESIAS: It will happen – I wrap it in silence – even then . . .

OEDIPUS: Ought you not to tell me what will happen?

TEIRESIAS: I won't say any more. Burst with anger, if you wish.

OEDIPUS: I am bursting with anger because of what I now understand. Yes. I think you are the one who planned this deed, and executed it, short of killing Laios with your own hand. And had you your eyes, I believe you would have done it on your own.

TEIRESIAS: Is that the truth? And I tell you that you ought to obey your own decree, and from this day forth never again speak to these people, or to me, because you are the noxious pollution of this land.

OEDIPUS: You spew out these words and hope to escape?

TEIRESIAS: I have escaped. The truth is strong. I have it.

OEDIPUS: Who taught it you? Not your craft.

TEIRESIAS: You did. You pushed me – unwilling – and I said it.

OEDIPUS: What? Say it again. I want to learn more.

TEIRESIAS: Didn't you understand before? You want more?

OEDIPUS: Not well enough. Say more.

TEIRESIAS: I say you are the murderer you seek.

OEDIPUS: You won't escape with these infamies.

TEIRESIAS: Shall I say more and increase your anger?

OEDIPUS: As much as you like – waste our time.

TEIRESIAS: I say that you – unaware, unconscious – without shame, have been consorting with your loved ones. And you do not see towards what troubles you are heading.

OEDIPUS: You think you can say all this and keep enjoying yourself?

TEIRESIAS: If there is any might in truth.

OEDIPUS: There is, except with you. You are blind in your ears, your mind and your eyes. There's nothing with you.

TEIRESIAS: You're pitiful to throw insults at me which you yourself will hear soon enough.

OEDIPUS: You're fed by darkness. How could you hurt me or anyone else who lives by the light?

TEIRESIAS: I do not need to bring on your fate. Apollo will do that: it is in his care.

OEDIPUS: Are these inventions yours or Kreon's?

TEIRESIAS: Kreon is not your calamity; you yourself are.

OEDIPUS: Wealth, power, extraordinary skill and a reputable life –
There envy lies in wait.
Watches you.
Now, for the sake of a throne I never craved, Kreon, once loyal, a friend from the beginning, Kreon now stalks, sly, and

plots to overthrow me – and secretly hires this juggler, this quack, this magus, completely blind as to his so-called skill but sharp-eyed when it comes to his own gain.

Yes, tell us about your wise prophecies –

What did you have to say when the riddling Sphinx-dog howled her rhapsodies?

How did you release the people? It wasn't any man who could solve the riddle; it needed divination. Where were your twittering birds then, where was your godly knowledge? But I, alone, I, Oedipus, knowing nothing, I stopped the Sphinx, learning the answer by thought, not by the twitching of birds.

And now you want to get rid of this man – me – so you can stand behind a Kreon-filled throne.

If you didn't look so decrepit, I'd make you suffer. Yes, you'd feel the full weight of your thoughts.

CHORUS: It seems to me this man and you as well, Oedipus, have spoken in anger. There is no need for this, but rather we need to consider how best we can be free of the God's pronouncement.

TEIRESIAS: You may be the master here, but there exists an equal right to reply. I have that right.

I am not your slave, but the God's. Nor am I Kreon's hireling.

And I say this: you call me blind, but you look with your eyes and can't even see where you're going – what troubles lie ahead.

Nor do you see where you live, or with whom. Do you even know your parents? And you don't know that you are abhorrent to your own – both below and on this earth. And a double-lashed curse, from your mother and your father, will one day – with a swift and terrible tread – chase you from this land – You see now, you see straight, but then darkness.

There will not be space enough in this whole region to hold your cries, no, your tears will lap the slopes of Kithairon, when you understand your marriage, this haven you sailed into – seemingly lucky.

14

No haven at all.
And you do not sense the quantity of other troubles swooping
down on you, making you the equal of your children.
Scoff. Hurl your insults at me, at Kreon –
No mortal before you will have been so miserably ground
down as you.

OEDIPUS: Do I have to listen to any more? Why aren't you dead?
Turn away, turn back.

TEIRESIAS: I wouldn't have come if you hadn't called me.

OEDIPUS: If I'd known I'd hear such moronic words, I'd have
asked you not to hurry.

TEIRESIAS: I seem mad to you, but I'm wise to your parents, those
who gave you birth.

OEDIPUS: Which? Wait. Which mortal gave me birth?

TEIRESIAS: The day that begets you also destroys you.

OEDIPUS: You can speak only riddles and obscurities.

TEIRESIAS: Aren't you the best qualified to read them?

OEDIPUS: Laugh. You can't belittle my accomplishments.

TEIRESIAS: Chance – and chance ruined you.

OEDIPUS: It doesn't matter how I did it, as long as I saved the city.

TEIRESIAS: I'm going now. Lead me, child.

OEDIPUS: Yes, lead him away. I'll feel lighter when you're gone.

TEIRESIAS: I'm going. I'm not afraid of you and I'll say what I
have to say to you. You cannot destroy me. And I tell you
this. The man you seek with your threatening
proclamations, claiming to instigate a long search for the
murderer of Laios, that man is here. Believed to be an alien,
but he will be revealed a native. Theban. And he will not
rejoice at this fact. Once he saw; now he will be blind. He
was rich; he will turn beggar, tapping his pitiable way on the
hard ground of foreign soil. Father and brother of his own
children; son and husband of the same woman. Mingling his
seed in the same place as the father he murders. Go inside;
examine this. And if you find I have lied, then say I don't
understand prophecy.

SECOND CHORUS

CHORUS

Who?
Who has committed the unspeakable?
Bloody hands.
Let him flee,
fast on his feet,
a galloping horse: watch the foam lace
his neck –
The son of Zeus glares at him.
The Fates pursue him,
relentless.

Track him down.
Track down this troubled, muddied
man.
That's what the message means.
I see him in a wood, in a cave,
bereaved, alone, shirking the oracles,
but they're always there, around him,
encircling, tightening.

Terrible.
This prophet upsets me.
I can't agree, I can't deny.
I never heard of a quarrel between the Thebans
and our master, the son of Polybos.
And Oedipus is popular. I cannot go
against his reputation, for the sake of
a death long ago, because of a remote
tale.

Zeus and Apollo know. Does the
prophet know? We can't be sure.
Another man could be wiser.

I'd want more proof, before I sided
against Oedipus. That riddling, singing
girl was worsted in combat with him;
he was good to the city; I can't
believe he is evil.

SECOND EPISODE

KREON: Men of the city, I've become aware of the terrible things our ruler Oedipus has been saying about me. It is unbearable. If I have harmed him in any way, by words or actions, I don't want to live any more. It's much more than a mere personal injury to be called harmful to the city, to my friends, and to you.

CHORUS: Perhaps there was more anger than judgement when those words came out.

KREON: But did he say it was my idea to persuade the prophet to spread lies?

CHORUS: It was said, perhaps without judgement.

KREON: Was his eye clear, his mind sane when he hurled that accusation at me?

CHORUS: I don't know. I don't look too closely at those in power. (OEDIPUS *comes on.*)

OEDIPUS: What are you doing here?
How dare you show yourself, murderer – would-be robber of my power. Tell me, did you think me a coward, or merely stupid, to make such plans?
Did you think you could creep up on me and I wouldn't notice? How foolish could you be, to seek to rule without wealth, without friends. Don't you know power requires popular support, money?

KREON: Do this. Listen to me. Learn; then judge.

OEDIPUS: A clever speech; I have nothing to learn. I have found you my enemy, an oppression.

KREON: Something I can explain –

OEDIPUS: Something you need not say: that you're not bad.

KREON: If you think obstinacy is desirable, you are mistaken.

OPIDUS: If you think wronging your kin is justifiable, you are mistaken.

KREON: That is well said, but teach me in what way I have wronged you.

OEDIPUS: Did you or did you not advise me to send for that magnificent prophet.

KREON: Yes, and I hold to that advice.

OEDIPUS: How long is it since Laios . . .

KREON: Did what? I don't understand.

OEDIPUS: Disappeared mysteriously by violent hands.

KREON: A long time ago, measured . . .

OEDIPUS: Was this prophet then exercising his craft?

KREON: Equally wise, equally honoured.

OEDIPUS: Did I come to his mind then?

KREON: Not when I was there.

OEDIPUS: And you were not able to search for the murderer?

KREON: We inquired; we heard nothing.

OEDIPUS: And so, why didn't this wise man say something then?

KREON: I don't know, and when I don't know I like to keep quiet.

OEDIPUS: You know this and you can say it.

KREON: What? If I know, I will.

OEDIPUS: That if he were not in league with you he wouldn't have called me the killer of Laios.

KREON: You know if he is saying these things. But now you must answer me as I have answered you.

OEDIPUS: I'll answer, but I will not be trapped as the murderer.

KREON: Didn't you marry my sister?

OEDIPUS: I can't deny it.

KREON: You rule this land with her.

OEDIPUS: I give her whatever she wants.

KREON: And I am equal to you both?

OEDIPUS: And this makes you an evil friend.

KREON: Not if you were to follow my reasoning. Consider this first. Why would anyone want to rule subject to fear when he can enjoy the same power and sleep soundly? I don't wish to be a ruler, but only to have the advantages of a ruler: that is prudent. Now I have whatever I want from you; as a ruler I would do what I had to – not always a pleasant task. I have power, I have painless influence, why should I wish to rule? I want riches, good things; all men wish me well, greet me. Anyone who wants you seeks me out: I am their hope. Why should I give all that up for something else? Finally, if you think I have plotted with the prophet, why don't you send to the Oracle and see if I reported what it said correctly. And if you find me guilty, I'll be condemned twice, once by you, once by myself. But don't condemn me with no more than a private suspicion.

CHORUS: He spoke well. He took care. It's dangerous to think too quickly.

OEDIPUS: When someone creeps stealthily upon me, I must be quick to stop him. If I stand still, inactive, he will succeed and I will fail.

KREON: What do you want to do? Exile me from this land?

OEDIPUS: Not at all. I want your death, not your escape. You will be an example of what happens to the envious.

KREON: You won't believe me? You are not thinking carefully.

OEDIPUS: I am thinking for myself.

KREON: You should think of me equally.

OEDIPUS: You are bad.

KREON: What if you have no judgement?

OEDIPUS: I must rule.

KREON: Even rule badly?

OEDIPUS: Oh city, city.

KREON: I belong to this city too.

CHORUS: Stop, lords. Jokasta comes here. None too soon. She can settle this.

JOKASTA: You fools, why this senseless argument?
Aren't you ashamed of airing a private quarrel when this country is so stricken?
Go back to your palace, and you, Kreon, to your house, and don't turn a petty grief into a great one.

KREON: Sister, your husband Oedipus condemns me to one of two evils: exile or capture and death.

OEDIPUS: I have caught him plotting evilly against me.

KREON: (*With a gesture to the gods*) May I never find happiness, may I die accursed, if I have done any of the things he says.

JOKASTA: You must believe him, Oedipus, out of respect for the oath he has now sworn to the gods, for my own sake and for that of these people as well.

CHORUS: Take heed, lord, think carefully, relent, we pray you.

OEDIPUS: You want me to yield?

CHORUS: Respect a man who was never thought a fool before and who is now ennobled by his oath.

OEDIPUS: Do you know what you ask?

CHORUS: I know.

OEDIPUS: Say it – clearly.

CHORUS: He is a friend, he has sworn an oath. Do not dishonour him because of an obscure rumour.

OEDIPUS: Then you're asking for my own death, my own exile.

CHORUS: By the sun, god of gods, that isn't so. It would be the last thing in my mind, but I am in despair. This land wastes away, tears at my heart – and now there's this new quarrel to add to our old troubles.

OEDIPUS: Let him go then, even if it means my certain death, my dishonourable exile. Your words, not his, bring on my pity. He will be hated, wherever he is.

KREON: You yield without grace, your anger exceeds all bounds. Such natures oppress themselves.

OEDIPUS: Leave me. Go.

KREON: I'm going – misunderstood by you, but still the same man as I was for these people.

CHORUS: Woman, why delay? Take this man back to the palace.

JOKASTA: Tell me first how this misfortune came about.

CHORUS: Words bred suspicion – and there injustice feeds –

JOKASTA: On both sides?

CHORUS: Yes.

JOKASTA: What words?

CHORUS: Enough, enough. I think about our land. Let it stop where it started.

OEDIPUS: You see how it goes; you mean well, but you blunt my resolve and you make me weak.

CHORUS: Lord, I will say it again and again. I would be insane, totally without judgement, to let you go – you who once piloted this beloved land through distraught times and now might guide us to safety again.

21

THIRD EPISODE

JOKASTA: Tell me, my lord, for the gods' sakes, what has caused such a rage.

OEDIPUS: I will. I honour you above all.
It is Kreon – and his plots.

JOKASTA: Tell me clearly how the quarrel began.

OEDIPUS: He says I am established as the murderer of Laios.

JOKASTA: He knows this himself, or he learned it from someone?

OEDIPUS: He sent the ill-omened prophet, so that he might keep his own mouth clean.

JOKASTA: Absolve yourself, Oedipus, and learn why no mortal can ever be infallible in the art of prophecy. I'll prove this to you.
An oracle came to Laios once, not necessarily from Apollo himself, but from one of his priests, and it said that his fate was to die at the hands of the child born to us both.
And now they say that Laios was murdered by foreign robbers at the fork where three paths meet.
And anyway, the child hadn't been alive three days before Laios fastened his ankles with pins and had him thrown on to a mountain well away from any path.
And so Apollo did not make this happen: the child did not become a murderer and Laios did not suffer the terrible fate he feared at the hands of his child. And yet these things were foreseen – and so don't heed them. When the God wants something to happen, he will reveal it himself.

OEDIPUS: My soul – my mind –
What upheavals – as I listen to you, my wife.

JOKASTA: What thought turns you so –

OEDIPUS: I thought I heard you say that Laios was killed at the meeting of three roads.

JOKASTA: It was said – it still is.

OEDIPUS: Where did this happen?

JOKASTA: The land is called Phokis. The road branches in two; one road leads to Delphi, the other to Daulia.

OEDIPUS: How much time has passed since all this happened?

22

JOKASTA: We heard about it shortly before you were proclaimed our ruler.

OEDIPUS: Oh God, what will you do with me?

JOKASTA: What is it, Oedipus? What disturbs you so?

OEDIPUS: Don't ask now. What was Laios's bearing like? How old was he?

JOKASTA: Tall – hair lightly silvered. Not unlike you in shape.

OEDIPUS: Ah, me.
And I hurled dread curses at myself – then – unknowing.

JOKASTA: What are you saying? I look at you – shrink back – fear –

OEDIPUS: Oh, despair – did the prophet see after all?
Tell me one thing more – and I'll have proof.

JOKASTA: This fear – but I will say what I know.

OEDIPUS: Did he go with a small escort or with the retinue that befits a king?

JOKASTA: There were five. One was a herald. Laios was in a chariot.

OEDIPUS: *Aiai, aiai.*
All is revealed –
Who told you this?

JOKASTA: A servant, the only one who survived.

OEDIPUS: Is he in the palace now?

JOKASTA: No. When he came back and saw you in power and Laios dead, he begged me to send him to the country, so that he could be far away from all sight of the city. I sent him. He was a good man, even though a slave, he was worth granting such a request, even more.

OEDIPUS: Could he come to us, quickly?

JOKASTA: Yes, but what for?

OEDIPUS: I fear for myself. I have said too much. I want to see him.

JOKASTA: He will come, but am I not worthy to learn of your burdens, lord?

OEDIPUS: You will. Who better than you? And my hopes have come to this –
My father was Polybos from Korinth, my mother the Dorian Merope. I was brought up as the first citizen of the city until a

23

chance encounter, rather strange, worthy of wonder, but
perhaps not worthy of my own reaction –
A man at a banquet, filled with too much wine said – drunk
– said I was not the true son of my father. I restrained
myself then, despite my distress, but the next day I went to
my mother and father and questioned them. They were
furious at the man who had let such words escape him.
They reassured me, but I was vexed – it remained – the
insult rooted, grew. And unknown to my mother and father,
I went to the Oracle.
Apollo sent me away ignorant as to that matter, but he
brought forth terrible utterances concerning me. He said that
I would intermingle with my mother, that my family would
be abhorrent to the sight of men, and that I would be the
murderer of my own father.
Having heard all this, I fixed my route by the stars to get as
far away as possible from Korinth, and keep these terrible
predictions from being realized. I was walking. I came to the
region where you say Laios died. And to you, my wife, I will
tell the truth.
I was coming down the road, near the meeting of the three
roads, the fork – when I met the herald – and a man on board
a chariot, as you say. The herald and the man in the chariot
ordered me aside. The driver jostled me – I struck him in
anger. The old man saw this, and as the chariot came beside
me, he struck me with a double goad. I retaliated, and struck
him with my stick. He rolled out of the chariot.
And then I killed them all.
And if that man had the blood of Laios in him, who would be
more abject than the man you see here? What man would be
more revolting to the gods? A man who might not be received
in anyone's house by strangers or by the citizens. The man
who must never be spoken to, but driven out of the city. It
was I who called down these curses on that man.
Laios. When I touch anything of this man, put my hand on
his bed, the defilement – the horror – if it is also the hand that
killed him.

Am I evil?
Unholy, defiled?
Must I flee? And fleeing, never again set foot upon my own
land? In marriage, am I to wed my mother? Kill my father
Polybos, who nurtured me? Can the god who brings these
things to pass be called anything but a cruel god?
Forbid, forbid, you holy, chaste and fearful gods, that I
should see that day.
No. I will walk away from mortals, vanish – before I suffer
such calamity.

CHORUS: We shrink in fear from these things, lord, but we have
hope until you find the man who was there.

OEDIPUS: Yes. Hope.
I can wait for this man to come from the country.

JOKASTA: But when he comes, what then? Why this haste?

OEDIPUS: This: if he says the same things as you then I can escape
this suffering.

JOKASTA: But what? What did you hear from me?

OEDIPUS: You told me he said several robbers killed Laios. One is
not the same as several.
If he still says there were several robbers, then I didn't kill
him. But if he says clearly that there was one single man, then
the evidence tips against me.

JOKASTA: That is what he said. He can't deny it now. The city
heard it, not I alone. And even if he turns away from this
story now, even then the Oracle would not be correct,
because Apollo said that Laios would be killed by my child.
That unfortunate being could not have killed him since he
himself died long before.
And so I would not look to divination for help with the past,
the present or the future.

OEDIPUS: Yes, but send someone to summon this man.

JOKASTA: I'll send for him instantly. Now let's go into the palace.
There is nothing I would not do for you.

THIRD CHORUS

CHORUS

I ask this of fate: purity in word and deed.
And especially: obedience to the laws.
The laws are sublime
born not of the earth, but in the heavens.
Laws never slacken, never sleep,
never grow old –
godly, mighty, impregnable laws.

Hubris breeds the tyrant.
Hubris fills itself with vanity,
misjudgement. It scrambles up, up, up,
and then tumbles down, down to the
inevitable abyss. That's Necessity. No
foothold there for anyone.

Now, if this struggle is good for the
city, then I pray God be my protector.

But the one
who speaks and acts haughtily – without
concern for justice, without reverence
for those sacred nooks of the gods –
let a terrible fate seize that man,
because he is arrogant,
foolish, greedy. Yes,
let a bad fate chew him to bits.
Let him not be overlooked by an angry
god. No, don't let him ever boast he
can go unpunished,
because if he can, why am I here? Why
do I speak? Dance?
And now, I will no longer go to Delphi
unless I find some sense in all this.

Zeus, master of all, who hears
everything, Zeus, notice this: the
oracles concerning Laios are melting
away, sliding into darkness, going
silent.

Apollo is without honour
and what is sacred vanishes.

JOKASTA: Lords of this country:
It occurred to me to come here to the temples of the gods,
with these wreaths and with incense.
Oedipus is in turmoil. He no longer judges with the skill of
his experience but he believes whoever speaks, especially if
the words are fearful. I cannot help him or advise him, and so
I have come to you, Apollo, with these offerings: help us,
release us. As
we watch him, in his panic, lose the helm of this land.
MESSENGER: Can you tell me, strangers, where is the palace of
Oedipus? And do you know where I might find him?
CHORUS: This is his palace. He is inside, but here is his wife and
the mother of his children.
MESSENGER: May she be happy and fulfilled, this wife who has
borne him children.
JOKASTA: And you too, stranger, because of your gracious words.
But what is the meaning of your presence?
MESSENGER: Good things for your husband.
JOKASTA: What? Where have you come from?
MESSENGER: From Korinth. And what I have to say will please
you, but it will pain you as well.
JOKASTA: What is it, this double-edged tiding?
MESSENGER: Korinth proclaims Oedipus its king.
JOKASTA: What? Isn't Polybos still in power?
MESSENGER: No. Death holds him.
JOKASTA: What did you say? The father of Oedipus is dead?
MESSENGER: If I am lying, I hope to die.
JOKASTA: (*To a servant*) Go in now and tell this to your master.
Oh prophecies, where are you now? Oedipus fled this man –
afraid he would kill him. And now this man has died in the
course of chance and not by Oedipus's hand at all.
OEDIPUS: Beloved wife Jokasta, why did you send for me?
JOKASTA: Listen to this man, and think again about so called
prophecies from the gods.
OEDIPUS: Who is he? What does he have to say to me?
JOKASTA: From Korinth, saying your father is dead.
OEDIPUS: What do you say, stranger? Tell me yourself.

MESSENGER: I'll say it clearly: the man – your father – is known to
  be dead.

OEDIPUS: The result of a plot? Or through illness?

MESSENGER: A small sinking of the scale kills old bodies.

OEDIPUS: And so the poor man declined from illness?

MESSENGER: And old age.

OEDIPUS: Fie then, why would anyone regard Apollo's hearth, or
  the screeching of the birds above, whose guidance made me
  believe I would kill my father. He died. He lies hidden under
  the earth. I did not brandish a spear – no, I did not kill him –
  unless it was his longing for me that destroyed him. In that
  sense, yes, he might have died because of me. But Polybos
  takes these oracles down to Hades with him. They are worth
  nothing.

JOKASTA: Didn't I tell you that a long time ago?

OEDIPUS: Yes, but I was lost in my fears.

JOKASTA: Don't let your spirit feed on these any more.

OEDIPUS: How can I not fear the bed of my mother?

JOKASTA: How can a man fear the accidents of chance?
  No one has access to the future. It is best not to plan too
  carefully but to live as well as one can. Do not fear marriage
  to your mother. Many men in their dreams have bedded their
  mother. The one who does not take any of this too seriously
  bears life more lightly.

OEDIPUS: This would have been well said if she were not still alive.
  But she lives, and whatever you say, I must fear.

JOKASTA: Surely the tomb of your father brings relief.

OEDIPUS: I am afraid of the living.

MESSENGER: Who is this woman you fear?

OEDIPUS: Merope, old man. Who lived with Polybos.

MESSENGER: What is it you fear about her?

OEDIPUS: A terrible prophecy of the gods.

MESSENGER: Can it be told? Or must no one know?

OEDIPUS: Apollo once said I would intermingle with my mother,
  and spill my father's blood with my own hands. It was
  because of this I left Korinth long ago. And yet, the faces of
  one's parents are sweet to behold.

MESSENGER: And it was to avoid these things you became an exile?

OEDIPUS: I did not want to kill my father, old man.

MESSENGER: Why have I not released you of this fear, since I came with good intentions?

OEDIPUS: You would find favour with me.

MESSENGER: Yes, I came for that, to gain some benefit when you go back to Korinth.

OEDIPUS: I will not go near my parents.

MESSENGER: Noble child, you don't know what you're doing.

OEDIPUS: What? Teach me, by the gods.

MESSENGER: If you avoid your home because of these things.

OEDIPUS: I am afraid the prophecy will prove true.

MESSENGER: That you should be guilty of a blood crime towards your parents?

OEDIPUS: Yes, I have always feared this.

MESSENGER: In all justice, you have nothing to fear.

OEDIPUS: How not, if I am the child of these parents.

MESSENGER: You were never related to Polybos.

OEDIPUS: What are you saying? Polybos fathered me.

MESSENGER: No more than the man you see standing here, the same.

OEDIPUS: How can a progenitor be the same as a stranger?

MESSENGER: He did not father you; nor did I.

OEDIPUS: Then why did he call me his child?

MESSENGER: He once took you from my hands.

OEDIPUS: How could he love me as his own, coming from other hands?

MESSENGER: He could because of his own childlessness.

OEDIPUS: And you, did you buy me? Or stumble upon me?

MESSENGER: I found you in the wooded slopes of Kithairon.

OEDIPUS: Why were you travelling in those places?

MESSENGER: I was looking after mountain flocks.

OEDIPUS: Were you a shepherd, or a vagabond for hire?

MESSENGER: Your saviour too, at that time, child.

OEDIPUS: You took me to save me from what?

MESSENGER: Your ankles would tell you that.

OEDIPUS: Ah, that terrible pain of old.

MESSENGER: I loosed your fettered ankles.

OEDIPUS: A shame I carry from my infancy.

MESSENGER: It was an accident that gave you your name.

OEDIPUS: Who did this? The gods? My mother? My father?

MESSENGER: I don't know. The man who gave you to me would know better.

OEDIPUS: You took me from someone else? You didn't chance upon me?

MESSENGER: No, another shepherd gave you to me.

OEDIPUS: Who is he? Can you tell me?

MESSENGER: He was probably one of Laios's men.

OEDIPUS: Who ruled this land long ago?

MESSENGER: Exactly. He was his herdsman.

OEDIPUS: Is the man still alive? Can I see him?

MESSENGER: The people here would know best.

OEDIPUS: Is there anyone here who knows this man? Either in the countryside, or here? Make him known to me.
The time has come to uncover all this.

CHORUS: I think he is none other than the man out in the country whom you were searching for earlier. Jokasta can tell us more.

OEDIPUS: Wife, the man we were seeking before . . . is this the man he speaks of?

JOKASTA: Why ask him? Don't waste a thought on it; it's senseless.

OEDIPUS: I cannot, with all these signs, refuse to bring my family to light.

JOKASTA: By the gods, if you care for your life, don't search this out –
It is enough that I am ill.

OEDIPUS: Be sure that even if I am the son of slaves, indeed from generations of slaves, it would not therefore mean you were basely born.

JOKASTA: Listen to me, I beg you. Don't pursue it.

OEDIPUS: I can't listen if you tell me not to find these things out.

JOKASTA: I know what I am saying. My advice is good.

OEDIPUS: This good advice of yours has caused me pain for a long
    time.
JOKASTA: Unlucky man. May you never know who you are.
OEDIPUS: Someone go and bring this herdsman to me. Let this
    woman enjoy her wealthy family undisturbed.
JOKASTA: *Eeou, eeou.*
    Ill-fated – that is the only word I have for you.
    And now nothing more ever again.
CHORUS: Why has she gone, Oedipus, cracking with grief? This
    silence –
    I fear terrible things will burst forth.
OEDIPUS: Let her crack. As for me, however humble, I want to
    know my genesis. As a woman, she may think great things of
    herself and feel ashamed of my obscure descent. I will not
    feel humiliated. I will call myself the child of chance. I am of
    that mother, and my brothers are the months of the year –
    who have sometimes cast me down and sometimes raised me
    to greatness. And having sprung of such parentage, I would
    not be another man in order to remain ignorant of where I
    came from.

FOURTH CHORUS

CHORUS

If I am a prophet – if I have
clear judgement – then
tomorrow, by the full moon,
you will be revealed Oedipus's
countryman, mountain of
Kithairon – Yes, his nurse, his
mother, and we will celebrate
you in dance because of the
favours you granted my ruler.

oh Kithairon

May this please you, Phoibus
Apollo.

ieeie Phoibe

Who, child, gave you birth?
Who of the nymphs came too
close to Pan? Or was it one
beloved of Apollo? Apollo,
who loves the high mountain
pastures?

tis se teknon, tis
s'etikte tan makraionon . . .
e se g'eunateira tis Loxiou

Or was it Hermes of Kyllene?
Or Bakchos: frenzied dancing
over the mountain peaks – he
receives you, delighted, from a
dark-eyed nymph.

ho Kullanas anasson
ho Baccheios Theos

tis se . . . tis s'etikte

33

OEDIPUS: Although I have never seen him I believe I recognize the herdsman we are seeking.

CHORUS: I know him well. He was a loyal shepherd to Laios.

OEDIPUS: First, I ask you, Korinthian, is this the man you spoke of?

MESSENGER: That's him.

OEDIPUS: Old man, look at me and answer all the questions I ask. Did you belong to Laios?

SERVANT: I was not bought. I was born into his household.

OEDIPUS: Where did you live? What did you do?

SERVANT: Most of the time, I looked after the herds.

OEDIPUS: In what area, usually?

SERVANT: Sometimes it was Kithairon, sometimes somewhere else, not far from there.

OEDIPUS: And do you know this man? Did you meet him there?

SERVANT: Doing what? Which man?

OEDIPUS: This man here. Have you ever associated with him?

SERVANT: Not so I can call him to mind quickly, no.

MESSENGER: Nothing to be surprised at, master. But I will make him remember. I know he can recall the time when we were both in Kithairon. He looked after two flocks. I had one. We spent three seasons together and in the winter I drove my flocks into my folds and he drove his into Laios's pens. Did these things happen as I tell them or not?

SERVANT: You speak the truth, but it was a very long time ago.

MESSENGER: And now tell me, do you remember at that time giving me a child so that I might raise it myself?

SERVANT: What's this? Why inquire?

MESSENGER: Here he is, good friend, this is the one who was young then.

SERVANT: Get away. Can't you keep quiet?

OEDIPUS: Don't beat him, old man. It's your words that will bring down a beating, not his.

SERVANT: How have I done wrong, master?

OEDIPUS: By saying nothing about the boy in this inquiry.

SERVANT: He doesn't know what he's talking about. He's fretting over nothing.

OEDIPUS: If you won't speak as a favour, we'll make you by force.

SERVANT: By the gods, don't torment an old man.

OEDIPUS: Someone quickly twist his hands behind his back.

SERVANT: Why, unfortunate, what do you wish to learn?

OEDIPUS: Is it you who gave him the child we're inquiring after?

SERVANT: I did. If only I'd died that day.

OEDIPUS: You will now if you don't speak the truth.

SERVANT: And if I do I am destroyed.

OEDIPUS: It seems to me this man is bent on delays.

SERVANT: No, I said it already, I gave it to him a long time ago.

OEDIPUS: Where did you take him from? Your own house or another's?

SERVANT: By the gods, master, don't inquire further.

OEDIPUS: You'll die if I have to ask again.

SERVANT: He was born in Laios's household.

OEDIPUS: A slave? Or kindred to Laios?

SERVANT: Oh, what terrible things I'm about to say.

OEDIPUS: And I to hear. But I will hear them all the same.

SERVANT: He was said to be the child of Laios, but your wife inside can tell you more.

OEDIPUS: She gave you the child?

SERVANT: Yes, lord.

OEDIPUS: For what purpose?

SERVANT: To kill it.

OEDIPUS: Having given birth to it?
Misery.

SERVANT: She was afraid of some bad prophecies.

OEDIPUS: Which ones?

SERVANT: It was said he would kill his parents.

OEDIPUS: How could you give him to this man then?

SERVANT: I took pity, master. I thought he would take him to his own land. But he saved him for the greatest troubles. And if you are the man he says you are, then you were born with an ill-fate.

OEDIPUS: *Eeou, eeou*

35

It all comes clear.
Light, let this be the last time I look on you.
I
who ought not to have been born the son I was, who ought
not to have married the woman I did, who ought not to have
killed those I did.

FIFTH CHORUS

CHORUS

Generations of mortals,
I count your life as nothing
For what man wins more than
a shadow of good fortune,
shadow that fades, fades away,
I hold up your
fate
as paradigm,
reckless Oedipus,
and I judge
no mortal happy.

eeoh
geneai broton
hos humas isa kai
to meden zosas
enarithmo
tis gar
tis aner pleon
tas
eudaimonias pherei
e tosouton hoson
dokein
kai doxant'apoklinai

He aimed highest,
he had luck and happiness,
wealth,
yes, Zeus, he slew the crooked-
clawed oracle-singing maiden.
He rose in our city, a bulwark
against death.

And so, Oedipus, we called you our
king, and we honoured you and you
ruled over magnificent Thebes.

And now who is more abject, more
cursed,
whose life has twisted more painfully
than yours,
renowned Oedipus?

That haven: as son,
as father, as bridegroom.
How is it the place
where you father sowed his seed didn't cry out
in horror?

Time sees all and found you out.
This marriage against all marriage,
bringing forth children there where
the father had been born.
Child of Laios,
I wish I'd never seen you. I lament, I
cry out.
Let me tell the truth.
It was you who brought me back to life.
Because of you I slept soundly again
and now you return me to darkness.

FIFTH EPISODE

MESSENGER: Honourable people of this land, if you are still
concerned with the house of the Labdakids, prepare
yourselves to see, to hear – ah, prepare yourselves for grief.
For all the rivers of the world, not the Danube, nor the Rion,
could cleanse this house of what lies hidden, what's seen to
be revealed, evils voluntary and involuntary, and surely the
worst of them is the suffering that has been self-inflicted.

CHORUS: We are bowed down by so much suffering already. What
are you saying now?

MESSENGER: To put it simply and quickly, the godly Jokasta is
dead.

CHORUS: Ah, ill-fated woman. How?

MESSENGER: Herself. By herself.
I didn't see everything. I'll tell what I saw.
In a passion of anger she ran into the hall.
Made straight for the bridal chamber.
Tearing her hair with the fingers of both hands,
went in, bolted the doors from inside.
Calls on Laios, long-time-dead Laios –
This memory: his seed, his offspring, cause of death and now
child-maker himself, breeding abominable offspring – and so
she gives birth to her husband and from this child-husband,
other children.
Abomination.
But now Oedipus bursts in. Shouting. We look at him,
stumbling, begging for a sword.
Asks us where he can find the wife-not-a-wife. And the
mother whose womb doubled for himself and for his
children.
And a god must have heard him – we kept away – and
seemed to beckon him, and with a terrible shout he rushed
to the double doors, forced the bolts and fell into the room.
And there we see the woman, hanging by the neck in a
twisted noose of swinging cords. He sees her, howls, howls
with a deep dread cry of misery, loosens the hanging rope

and when the poor woman was laid on the ground, then there were even worse things to see
because:
ripping her two golden brooches from the shoulders of her dress, he raises them up and strikes his eyeballs in their sockets.
Ranting they would not see what evil he was suffering, what evil he was doing,
but for the rest of time darkness would cover those it was not right for him to see, and not let him know those he had wanted to know.
He raved on and not once but several times struck his eyes.
Until the bloody eyeballs dangled over his chin. Dangled.
A hail of blood.
These just people were once happy, wealthy.
Now, today, lamentation, folly, death, shame, all the evils which can be named are present here.
None has been missed out.

CHORUS: And now? Does this unfortunate man have any respite?

MESSENGER: He shouts for the doors to be opened that he may reveal to all Thebans the patricide, his mother's husband, saying things I can't repeat and saying he will leave the land, but you'll see for yourselves, the doors are opening.

CHORUS: Terrible suffering.
The most terrible thing I have ever encountered.
What madness, unfortunate one, attacked you?
Which of the gods leapt on your fate with such destructive force?
Feu, feu
Unlucky. I can't look at you.
And yet, so many things to ask, to learn, to examine.

OEDIPUS: *Aiai, aiai.*
Unfortunate.
Where am I carried in the land, stricken?
Where does my voice sweep to? Oh destiny, where have you thrust me?

CHORUS: To a terrible place – unspeakable –
unwatchable.

OEDIPUS: Darkness.
The cloud came this way, inexorable, would not be
diverted –
Oimoi –
and more – more.
This piercing pain and the piercing memory of ill –

CHORUS: This is not surprising: redoubled cry for doubled
sorrow.

OEDIPUS: Ah, friend
you would look after a blind man.
Friends . . .
Feu, feu

CHORUS: Man of terrible deeds: how could you extinguish your
eyes?
What destiny drove you?

OEDIPUS: Apollo. It was Apollo, friend, who completes these
terrible things, this evil I must suffer.
But it was my hand that struck, not his.
What was there to see? What sweetness, where, to see?

CHORUS: As you say.

OEDIPUS: What was there to see? What left to love? And seeing, to
love?
Friend.
Take me away, the murderer of murderers, the cursed of the
cursed, and of humans the most hateful to the gods.

CHORUS: Your mind tortures you as much as your pain. How I
wish I'd never known you.

OEDIPUS: Death to the beggar who took me and rescued me!
Now I am without god – the child of unholy parents,
fertilizing her from whom I was myself born.
And if there is any worse evil anywhere to be committed, then
Oedipus will be guilty of that too.

CHORUS: I cannot say you have done the right thing: it might have
been better for you to die than be blind.

OEDIPUS: Don't teach me, don't tell me what I did was wrong.

If I had gone to Hades with my sight, how would I look upon
my father? And my mother?
Would the sight of my children have been pleasant?
Children born in this way –
And how could I look upon these walls, the towers, the
sacred statues of the gods, I, once the most noble child of
Thebes, revealed unholy by the gods.
I am supposed to look on the people of the city. No. If I could
pierce the sound from my ears I would do so.
Oh, to hear nothing, wall this body up, blind, deaf, in
darkness, in silence, in nothing.
Away from evil.
Why did you receive me, Kithairon? Why didn't you kill me
on the spot?
Then no humans would know my parentage.
Polybos, Korinth, you raised me to seem beautiful, and the
rot cankered underneath.
That meeting of roads, those woods – drank the blood from
my hands, blood of the father.
Oh marriage, marriage
gives me birth, then the same seed, grown, produces
others, fathers, brothers, children, incestuous blood, brides,
wives, mothers and all the deeds of shame, whatever they
are.
And so, far from the gods, hide me, kill me, throw me into
the sea.
Come, come touch this unhappy man.
Don't be afraid. My evils are mine and will infect no one but
me.

CHORUS: Kreon can do this or advise. He comes at the right time
as he alone is left to look after this land instead of you.

OEDIPUS: What can I say to him? How can he trust me?
I was no good to him before.

KREON: I am not here to mock, Oedipus, nor to reproach you
with your past evil. But you people, even if you no longer
respect humanity, respect the fire that lights this world. Do
not show such pollution uncovered, which neither the earth

42

nor the rain nor the light can bear. Take him into the house. For only the piety of the family makes it fit to see and hear such trouble.

OEDIPUS: By the gods, since you come, you the best of men, to me, the worst of men, listen to me. I speak for you, not for myself.

KREON: What do you want so desperately from me?

OEDIPUS: Expel me from this land as quickly as you can. Somewhere no human being will ever speak to me again.

KREON: I would do this, but I must first ask instructions from the God.

OEDIPUS: He has made it clear: the patricide must die.

KREON: It was so, but in our present distress, let us find out more clearly.

OEDIPUS: Will you ask, then, on behalf of this sorrowful man?

KREON: Yes, and you yourself will now have faith in the God.

OEDIPUS: And now let me beg you this and trust you to do it: her – chose her tomb and complete the rites owned to her – you will do this properly.

As for me – let me never be allowed to live in this city. Let me go to the hills, to Kithairon, my Kithairon, which my own mother and father designated as my grave. There let me die at last.

My children.

Don't concern yourself, Kreon, with my sons. They are men, they will live, wherever.

But my daughters, my daughters who were never far from me, wherever I sat, ate. Care for them, Kreon. And now, especially, let me touch them with my hands and let me cry, let me cry.

If I could touch them with my hands, then I would feel I held them as I did when I could see . . .

What am I saying?

I hear . . .

I hear them sobbing.

Kreon has pitied me and sent for my two beloved offspring? Is it so?

KREON: I knew what joy you had in them before.

OEDIPUS: Good fortune be yours, and for this act, a kind spirit protect you as it neglected me.

Children, where are you? Come here, come to these brotherly hands, hands that have put your father in this state – your father who could not see, could not learn where he came from. I cry for you both.

I can't see you now . . . I think of the life you will lead at the hands of men, the bitter life. What conversation with people of the city will you have? What festivals will you enjoy? No, you'll come home in tears.

And when it is time for you to marry, what man will ignore the insults that clothe you and risk the evil of offspring?

No one. You'll have to waste away, barren, unmarried. Kreon, child of Menoikeus, you are their father now. Don't let them wander the world as husbandless beggars. They are your kin, don't perceive them through my own evil. Pity them. Nod, lord, touch my hand, say yes. And you, children, let me only pray that when the moment comes, you be granted a better life than the father who sired you.

KREON: Enough now, enough tears. Go into the house.

OEDIPUS: I must obey – I don't want to.

KREON: There is a right time for everything.

OEDIPUS: When do I leave?

KREON: You are asking me for God's answer.

OEDIPUS: But I am hateful to the gods.

KREON: You will know soon enough – they may wish you to leave.

OEDIPUS: Take me away now.

KREON: Go, but leave the children.

OEDIPUS: Ah, no, don't take them away.

KREON: You can't rule over everything. Not now. All that you ruled over has left you.

CHORUS: Inhabitants of Thebes, here is Oedipus. He knew riddles, he was a man of power, few looked on him without

44

envy. See what calamities have come upon him.

And seeing this, how can we say anyone is happy until he has crossed to the other side without suffering.

OEDIPUS AT KOLONOS

PROLOGUE

Kolonos.

OEDIPUS: Child of the blind old man, Antigone, what country
have we reached, what city?

Who will receive the wandering Oedipus today?

From whom will he squeeze meagre gifts? I ask for little, I get
even less, but it suffices.

To be content is something I have learned with suffering,
with time, and, third, from innate nobility.

ANTIGONE: Father, careworn Oedipus, the towers of the city seem
far away –

This can only be a sacred place: matted with laurel, olive,
vine. And in the deepest thicket, a world of nightingales –
propitious song.

Sit on this unhewn stone.

You've travelled far for an old man.

OEDIPUS: Can you say where we are?

ANTIGONE: I would know Athens, but not this place.

I see a man coming to us; he's here. Speak to him.

OEDIPUS: Stranger, I hear from this girl, whose eyes serve herself
and me as well, that you have come fortuitously – to tell us –

STRANGER: Before you inquire after anything, leave this place.

This is a place not to be trodden upon; it's holy.

OEDIPUS: What is this place? Known to be of which god?

STRANGER: Not to be touched, not to be lived in.

It belongs to the fearful goddesses – goddesses of the Earth
and of the Dark.

OEDIPUS: What name shall I use when I pray to them?

STRANGER: Here they are called the all-seeing Eumenides.

Elsewhere, other names.

OEDIPUS: Let them receive this suppliant with grace. I will not
move from the ground where I sit.

STRANGER: What are you saying?

OEDIPUS: Here I meet my fate.

Tell me, what is this place to which we have come?

STRANGER: The whole place is sacred. Sacred to Poseidon and to the Titan Prometheus, bearer of fire.

The place you're treading on is called the Threshold of Brass: it is the pillar of Athens. In these fields near us, they bear the name of the horseman Kolonos, once their leader.

OEDIPUS: So some people do live here?

STRANGER: Yes, those that owe their name to the God.

OEDIPUS: Do they have a ruler, or are decisions taken by the people?

STRANGER: The city is ruled by a king.

OEDIPUS: Who is he who holds such power of word and deed?

STRANGER: He is called Theseus, the son of Aigeus.

OEDIPUS: Would a messenger go to him?

STRANGER: To say what? Ask him here?

OEDIPUS: From giving a little assistance he might derive great gain.

STRANGER: What can be gained from a blind man?

OEDIPUS: My words are not without sight.

STRANGER: You seem noble, despite your destiny. Stay. I will go and talk to the people here. They will decide. (*He goes.*)

OEDIPUS: Stern and fearful queens, it is your hearth I reach first in this land. Do not ignore the wishes of Apollo, nor my own.

It was Apollo who, when he proclaimed the list of troubles that were to befall me, promised that after a long time I would come to a final place where I would find the seat of the awesome gods.

And there my miserable life would turn. Then I would bring benefits to those who received me and ruin to those who drove me out. And he told me of signs, an earthquake, or thunder, or the lightning flashes of Zeus.

And now, austere goddesses, take in the austere wanderer and bring my life to its conclusion –

unless I still seem to be beneath such grace.

Or perhaps I still have not suffered enough?

Come, sweet daughters of darkness,

Come, city of Pallas Athene, honoured city –
Pity this shadow of Oedipus, no longer the man he once was.
(*The* CHORUS *comes on.*)
ANTIGONE: Here come some old men – to find you –
OEDIPUS: Hide me – let me hear them and decide . . .

FIRST CHORUS

CHORUS

hora

See. *tis ar ein*

Where is he? *pou naiei*

Where? *pou kurei ektopios sutheis*

Where has he fled, *ho panton, ho panton*

this man, *akorestatos*

this most reckless man?

Look around. Ask. Search him out.

A wanderer, *planatas, planatas*

a wandering old man, *tis ho presbus*

not from here,

a foreigner.

How else could he have come into these

woods, sacred, of the anger-prone

maidens?

When we go by,

we don't look.

We don't mention their names.

When we go by

it's in reverent silence.

And now someone has come.

No fear, no respect,

and I cannot find him.

FIRST EPISODE

OEDIPUS: (*Coming forward*) Here he is. Myself.

CHORUS: Dreadful sight
dreadful voice.

OEDIPUS: Don't, I beg you, look upon me as a law-breaker.

CHORUS: Guardian Zeus, who is this old man?

OEDIPUS: Not the most fortunate, or I would not be stumbling about, dependent on the loan of other eyes.

CHORUS: Listen, stranger, if you want to speak to me you will have to move from there and go where people are allowed. Until then, beware.

OEDIPUS: What shall I do, daughter?

ANTIGONE: We must obey the customs of the country, father.

OEDIPUS: Don't harm me if I trust you and move elsewhere.

CHORUS: You will never be removed against your will, old man.

OEDIPUS: Is this far enough?

CHORUS: Come forward a little.

OEDIPUS: Further?

CHORUS: Bring him this way, girl, you understand –
(ANTIGONE *does so.*)
There. Move no further than this rock –

OEDIPUS: Here?

CHORUS: Yes, stop.

OEDIPUS: Shall I sit?

CHORUS: Yes, on top of the rock.
Now you may rest . . . poor man.
(*Pause.*)
I'd ask from what country . . .

OEDIPUS: Strangers, I am without a city – but don't –

CHORUS: What would you forbid, old man?

OEDIPUS: Don't, don't ask me who I am.
Don't probe –

CHORUS: What do you mean?

OEDIPUS: Terrible birth.

CHORUS: Speak.

OEDIPUS: Ah, child, what shall I say?

CHORUS: What is your genesis, foreigner? Who was your father?

OEDIPUS: Ah, child, what will become of me?

CHORUS: Speak – you can't escape.

OEDIPUS: I'll speak. I have no means to hide.

CHORUS: You're delaying. Hurry.

OEDIPUS: Do you know of a child of Laios?

CHORUS: *Eeou.*

OEDIPUS: And the Labdakid family.

CHORUS: Oh God.

OEDIPUS: The pitiful Oedipus.

CHORUS: You are that man?

OEDIPUS: Don't be afraid of what I say . . .

CHORUS: Oh, oh, oh.

    Eeoh.

OEDIPUS: . . . of an ill-fate.

CHORUS: Oh, oh.

OEDIPUS: What now, daughter?

CHORUS: Get out of this country.

OEDIPUS: And your promise?

CHORUS: Get up, go, go away, leave my land. Don't make my city liable.

ANTIGONE: Compassionate strangers, pity me at least, I beg you, as I plead on behalf of my father.

Look on me as you would on one of your own – and let him find pity in you.

See, we stand before you as before gods. In the name of all that you love and of everyone you care for, have pity.

And

ask yourselves this.

Where is the mortal who can escape when it is the God who leads?

CHORUS: We pity you, yes, but we are afraid of the gods.

OEDIPUS: What has happened to the glory, the renown of Athens? They say Athens reveres the gods and welcomes foreigners in danger –

Athens claims to be the only city strong enough to defend them. Now it seems merely the sound of my name frightens you. It cannot be my body, nor my actions.

My actions –

I have suffered my actions, I did not commit them. I suffered and I reacted. Tell me, how was I evil when, knowing nothing, I did what I did? Even if I had known . . . But they knew – those who caused my suffering, wanted my death.

And now I beg you, by our gods, since you made me leave that protected place, save me –

You honour the gods, don't ignore them. You accepted me as a suppliant; watch over me now.

I have come, reverend, sacred, and I bring benefits to these citizens.

CHORUS: We will leave this to the rulers of the land.

ANTIGONE: Oh Zeus, what must I say?

OEDIPUS: What is it, child?

ANTIGONE: I see a woman riding towards us.

Yes, I am sure, it is Ismene.

(ISMENE *comes*.)

ISMENE: Doubly sweet greeting of father and sister –

I've shed tears searching for you and now I've found you, I can hardly see you through my tears.

OEDIPUS: Child, you're here?

ISMENE: Ill-fated father.

OEDIPUS: Touch me, child.

ISMENE: I touch you both.

OEDIPUS: Unlucky progeny –

ISMENE: Unfortunate lives –

OEDIPUS: The two of us?

ISMENE: And I the sorry third.

OEDIPUS: Why have you come, child?

ISMENE: As a messenger. I was the only one I could trust.

OEDIPUS: Where were your brothers when you needed this service?

55

ISMENE: They are where they are; terrible things –

OEDIPUS: Those two follow the customs of the Egyptians. There, the men stay inside and sit at the loom while the women go out to work and provide the food – And so your two brothers stay at home and they leave you to bear your father's burdens. She has wandered with me through the woods, barefooted, in the rain, the pounding heat. No thought of a hearth for her, only the toil of gathering scrap-food for her father. And you have been my faithful messenger, guardian of my interests in Thebes. What brings you here this time? You would not come empty-handed; you bear some new terror for me.

ISMENE: My own sufferings in finding you, father, I will not renew by telling – only the troubles surrounding your two sons. At first, they were urging Kreon to take the throne so that the city might no longer suffer the pollution – the curse on your house. But today, a god and an irreverent mind have brought these three-times ill-fated brothers into a terrible conflict; each one wants to win the right to rule and gain absolute power. And the youngest son has deprived the elder, Polyneikes, of the throne and driven him out of his country. It is now said that Polyneikes has gone to the plain of Argos and there gathered allies and soldiers –
And he believes they will conquer Thebes or else Thebes will sing its own victory.
These are not only words, father, but terrible deeds. As for when the gods will take pity on your sufferings, that is something I have not managed to learn.

OEDIPUS: Are you hoping the gods are watching over me – that I might one day be released?

ISMENE: Yes, because of the new prophecies, father – the recent oracles.

OEDIPUS: What has the Oracle said, child?

ISMENE: That men will search for you, either dead or alive, for their own safety.

OEDIPUS: What could they gain from such a man as I?

ISMENE: They say their power resides in you.

OEDIPUS: Now that I am no longer anything, I become a man?

56

ISMENE: The gods who destroyed you before would now set you right.

OEDIPUS: A waste to set an old man right, who was wrecked so young –

ISMENE: And it's because of this that Kreon comes here – imminently.

OEDIPUS: To do what, daughter? Be clear.

ISMENE: So that they might settle you near Thebes, where they would have power over you, but without your stepping into the land.

OEDIPUS: What benefit am I to them outside their gates?

ISMENE: Misfortune for them later if your tomb is not looked after.

OEDIPUS: No need of a god to understand that.

ISMENE: Because of that they want to keep you close, but powerless.

OEDIPUS: Will they bury me in Theban ground?

ISMENE: The spilling of kindred blood forbids this.

OEDIPUS: Then I will never let them take me.

ISMENE: This will cause grief to the Thebans.

OEDIPUS: In what way?

ISMENE: Because of your anger, when they take their stand by your tomb.

OEDIPUS: Whom have you heard these things from, child?

ISMENE: From those who went to hear the oracles.

OEDIPUS: Has any of my sons heard this?

ISMENE: Yes, both know it well.

OEDIPUS: And having heard this, these evil men find tyranny more desirable than the possibility of bringing me back to Thebes?

ISMENE: It hurts me to say these things, but they are so.

OEDIPUS: Then let the gods never extinguish their predestined conflict. And when they raise their spears against each other, may the outcome of this battle remain in my power.
And may this happen:
Let the one who now holds the sceptre and the throne lose it.
And let the one who has left the city, the exile, let him never

return.

For

not one of them, when I, their father, was dishonourably
driven from the land, not one of them kept me back – not one
of them defended me when I was being chased from house
and home. No, they watched as I was tossed out, declared an
exile.

You might say I myself wanted this and the city reasonably
granted my wish. It is true that on the day it all happened, my
spirit was boiling, and it would have pleased me to die,
stoned to death – with stone after stone.

At that time, no one complied, no one granted me this
respite.

Only later, when my distress was eased and I understood that
my spirit had been excessively harsh on my past failings, then,
then the city drove me out by force –
so long afterwards.

And those sons could have helped their father then, but they
did not choose to do it. And for the lack of one word, I was
made to wander for ever, an exile, a beggar – alien – always
outside.

From these two girls I receive sustenance, security, family
support. Those two preferred thrones, sceptres, and the
power of tyranny to their begetter.

No, I will never be their ally. They will derive no benefit from
the rule of Thebes.

Let them send Kreon, or anyone else in power.

But if you, strangers, join these revered and watchful
goddesses and defend me, you will provide your city with a
great saviour and give pain to my enemies.

CHORUS: You are worthy of pity, Oedipus, and your daughters as
well. But since you call yourself a saviour of Athens, let me
advise you as to what is right.

OEDIPUS: Good friend, I will do what you wish – you are this
alien's guide and advocate.

CHORUS: Propitiate the goddesses upon whose soil you
trespassed.

ISMENE: I will go and find all that is necessary and say these prayers. You, Antigone, watch over our father . . .

CHORUS: It is a fearful thing, stranger, to stir up troubles laid to rest long ago . . . And yet I am eager to hear . . .

OEDIPUS: What's this?

CHORUS: The sorry and seemingly intractable distress with which you tangled . . .

OEDIPUS: By the rules of hospitality, don't uncover those things I endured – beyond shame.

CHORUS: So many stories . . .
They never fade . . .
I so wish to hear the correct version . . .

OEDIPUS: *Oimoi.*

CHORUS: Do this, I beg you.

OEDIPUS: *Feu, feu.*

CHORUS: Comply. I did all you asked –

OEDIPUS: I bore the worst, strangers, none of these things was freely chosen by me.

CHORUS: In what way?

OEDIPUS: The city bound me to an evil bed – knowing nothing – ruin of marriage . . .

CHORUS: It was with a mother that you filled this infamous bed . . .

OEDIPUS: *Oimoi.*
Death to hear these things –
And these two girls of mine . . .

CHORUS: These girls . . .

OEDIPUS: These children, two abominations.

CHORUS: Oh Zeus.

OEDIPUS: Issued from the birth pangs of the same mother.

CHORUS: And so they are your children and . . .

OEDIPUS: Yes, the sisters of their father.

CHORUS: *Eeoh.*

OEDIPUS: *Eeoh.*
The turn, turnabout of countless ills.

CHORUS: Unfortunate man. And you shed blood . . .

OEDIPUS: What's this, what do you want to learn?

CHORUS: A father . . .

OEDIPUS: *Papai.*

A second stab, anguish on anguish.

CHORUS: You killed.

OEDIPUS: I killed. But there is to me . . .

CHORUS: What?

OEDIPUS: In all justice . . .

CHORUS: How so?

OEDIPUS: I will say –

I was caught in ruin.

I am pure before the law.

I came to this without knowing . . .

CHORUS: Here is our lord, Theseus, the son of Aigeus. Come to you at your request.

THESEUS: Your apparel and lamentable mien reveal who you are, Oedipus. I heard long ago how you gashed your own eyes. And – pitying you – I wish to learn from yourself what supplication you bring to the city and to myself, you and your unhappy companion.

Tell me –

You would have to describe the most terrible deeds for me to withdraw. I was once brought up an exile, like you, and I faced all the dangers that beset a foreigner, and beçause of this, I would never turn away a foreigner like you now, but would always help him.

I know I am only a man and have no greater security in the morrow than you do.

OEDIPUS: Theseus, your generosity in your brief discourse allows me to put my case in a few words.

THESEUS: Tell me, I long to hear.

OEDIPUS: I have come to donate my pitiful body to you as a gift, not goodly to look on

but the gains deriving from it are more powerful than a graceful form.

THESEUS: What gains do you purport to bring us?

OEDIPUS: You will learn this in time, not now.

THESEUS: But when will this offering be made manifest?

60

OEDIPUS: When I am dead and you have buried me.

THESEUS: Your wishes concern only your death. What about the rest of your life?

OEDIPUS: All comes together in that favour.

THESEUS: The favour you ask for is small –

OEDIPUS: Take care: the struggle is not small.

THESEUS: Are you talking about one between me and your sons?

OEDIPUS: They want me to crawl back to Thebes.

THESEUS: Is it not what you wish? It is not good for you to remain in exile.

OEDIPUS: When it was what I wanted, they refused.

THESEUS: Foolish – your anger is not helpful to you.

OEDIPUS: When you have learned my story, then chastise me. Until then, desist.

THESEUS: Tell me. I won't speak without knowledge.

OEDIPUS: I have suffered, Theseus, evil upon evil.

THESEUS: Are you speaking of the old misfortunes of your family?

OEDIPUS: No, no. These are known throughout the Greek world.

THESEUS: What are these ills that are more than a man can bear?

OEDIPUS: This: I have been turned out of my country by my own offspring. And I am never to return, because I am a patricide.

THESEUS: Then why would they come for you?

OEDIPUS: The Oracle compels them.

THESEUS: What suffering do they fear from the Oracle?

OEDIPUS: That of necessity they will be struck down by this country.

THESEUS: Why should any bitterness come between them and me?

OEDIPUS: Good friend, son of Aigeus, only the gods never become old, never die.

Time – dictator time – wrecks all else.

The might of the earth wastes away.

The strength of the body too.

Loyalty faith trust, all die, and treachery flourishes.

No spirit remains constant between men, between cities.

Soon

or perhaps later
the sweet becomes bitter and then loved again.

And so if between you and Thebes the days now pass in
pleasantness, infinite time brings on infinite days and nights,
in which, to the echo of a small word, a spear will smash the
concord of past days.

And then my sleeping corpse, hidden, cold, will drink their
hot blood, if Zeus is still Zeus and Apollo speaks true.

It is not right to speak of these mysteries.

Theseus, you will never say you received a useless dweller
when you took Oedipus in – unless the gods have lied to me.

CHORUS: Lord, this man shows himself willing to help our city.

THESEUS: Yes, who would reject the good will of such a man? I
will make him an ally, give him a share of our public hearth
and welcome him to the city.

And in reverence for his promises, I will establish him a
citizen.

And if it is his pleasure to remain here, then I charge you to
look after him.

Or he may want to come with me.

OEDIPUS: If it were right – but this is the place.

THESEUS: Where you will do what? I will not oppose you.

OEDIPUS: Where I will have power over those who threw me out.

THESEUS: Your association would then be a great gift.

OEDIPUS: But you must keep your promises.

THESEUS: Be assured, I am not the man to abandon you.

OEDIPUS: And I will not bind you with an oath as I would
someone untrustworthy.

THESEUS: An oath would not be more reliable than my word.

OEDIPUS: What will you do?

THESEUS: What are you so frightened of?

OEDIPUS: Men will come –

THESEUS: These will deal with them.

OEDIPUS: Beware you don't desert me.

THESEUS: Don't teach me what to do.

OEDIPUS: I have such fears –

THESEUS: My own heart knows no fear.

OEDIPUS: You don't know what threats –
THESEUS: I only know that no one will take you away from here by
force –
Even if I am not here myself, my name will protect you from
harm.

SECOND CHORUS

CHORUS

In this country of swift horses,
foreigner, you have found safe-dwelling.
Kolonos.
Full-throated nightingales
hide in the deep of wooded coombs.
Arbour dark with ivy,
garnished with fruit,
never trodden
but by the God.
No sun, no wind, no storm,
only Dionysos
dance-steps with his nurse-nymphs,
unstoppable
company of revellers.

Heavy with the drink of morning dew,
day after day the narcissus flowers,
crown of sorrow for the two goddesses,
and the crocus opens
petals like sunset.
Every day sleepless springs
sprinkle streams, spread rivers, feed
plains, swell the contours of the land . . .
land where the Muses are not silent,
land loved by Aphrodite,
light goddess hands on golden reins.

There is a plant
unknown in the Asian stretches
unknown even in the Peloponnese.
A plant that seeds itself
unconquered
scarecrow to alien spears:

the grey-green olive.
Feeds our children.
No wanton youth, no bitter grey-beard
can harm it, make it fruitless.
Zeus watches over it
with statesman care –
Athene scans it
with sharp grey eyes.
And there is more to celebrate.
Our horses, our yearlings, our sea
and
glorious gift of the sea god:
the bridle.
Here, on these streets, Poseidon taught us
to curb our horses
and to craft the oar,
glinting in the waves
in syncopation with
the centipede sea-nymphs.

SECOND EPISODE

ANTIGONE: This is a much-praised land. Let these bright words
now turn into deeds.

OEDIPUS: What new thing now, child?

ANTIGONE: Kreon comes this way.

OEDIPUS: Good friends, old men, only you can keep me safe.

CHORUS: You will be safe. Even if I am old, the strength of this
country is not.

KREON: Noble inhabitants of this land, I see by your eyes my
coming here has frightened you.

Please, have no fear and say nothing against me.

I have not come with any thought of force.

I am old and I know I am in the most powerful city of
Greece.

But I have been sent, old as I am, to persuade this man to
follow me to Thebes. I come not at the will of one man, but
at the request of all the citizens, because he is my kin – and as
his kin I have grieved for his sufferings more than any other
Theban.

Listen to me, Oedipus, yours has been a long, a painful road.
Come back to your home.

All the Thebans call on you, as they should in justice – and
none more than I.

For I am most grieved by your troubles, old man, seeing you
in this lamentable state, a foreigner, a beggar, and no other
help than this girl, who has fallen low indeed.

Oedipus, come back to Thebes, come back to your father's
land, say a friendly goodbye to Athens, as is meet, but respect
the rights of the country that nurtured you.

OEDIPUS: Daring.

Devious plans coil around your sham-noble words.

When I was ill with the troubles of my family, when it would
have been a joy to leave, you wouldn't oblige, you wouldn't
let me go.

But when I was sated with my anger,
when I found living at home had become sweet,

66

then
you threw me out.
And kinship mattered little to you then.
You see this city take me in and her citizens grant me
welcome and now you want to turn me back, coating harsh
thoughts in dulcet sounds.
That's you: good words, evil acts. But I will reveal you to
these people. You do not intend to bring me home, but to
place me on the edge of Thebes, somewhere, so the city will
be protected from any danger from this country.
No, Kreon. I will not protect the city. I will be your
tormentor, no more. As for my sons, they will win enough
land to be buried in.
Believe me, I know more about the affairs of Thebes than
you.

KREON: Unlucky man, time has not brought you wisdom. You're
a disgrace to old age.

OEDIPUS: Go away. I speak for these too. Don't spy on me here –
my destined haven.

KREON: I call these men to witness how you answer your kin. If I
ever take you –

OEDIPUS: And who could take me by force with these allies
nearby.

KREON: You will find you already have enough to weep about.

OEDIPUS: What makes you say that?

KREON: I've seized one of your daughters and sent her away. Now
I will take this one.

OEDIPUS: *Oimoi.*

KREON: You'll have more cause to weep soon.

OEDIPUS: You have my child?

KREON: And I'll have this one before long.

OEDIPUS: Strangers, what will you do? Will you betray me?
Won't you drive this impious man from the country?

CHORUS: Go, stranger, go away now, quickly.

KREON: I'll take the girl by force – if you won't agree to come.

ANTIGONE: *Oimoi.*
Misery.

67

Where can I escape to? Who will help me? What god? What men?

CHORUS: Stranger, what are you doing?

KREON: I won't touch that man, but she is one of my own.

OEDIPUS: Old men of this land!

CHORUS: Stranger, you are not acting justly.

KREON: It is just.

CHORUS: How?

KREON: I take what is mine –

(KREON *seizes* ANTIGONE.)

OEDIPUS: Oh city, city.

KREON: Take her away.

OEDIPUS: Misery, misery.

KREON: No more wandering for you now – brandishing your two crutches.

And since you want to triumph over your country and over your friends, triumph then.

Know this much: you've done yourself no good, not now, not in the past, by giving way to your anger, anger which always maims you.

OEDIPUS: May the powers of this place strengthen my voice to utter this curse: evil of evil men, who took away the eyes I relied on, when I had lost my own already, I call upon the god of the sun, the god who sees all things, to afflict you and your progeny with an old age such as mine –

KREON: I won't hold back any more.

I may be old, but I will take that man by force.

(THESEUS *enters*.)

THESEUS: What has happened? What is this shouting? You interrupted my sacrifice to Poseidon. Speak.

OEDIPUS: Kreon

has torn my two children – my only children – away from me.

THESEUS: Let one of my attendants go at once to the altars of Poseidon and order everyone, mounted and unmounted, to hurry to where the two main roads meet, so that the girls will not get beyond our borders.

68

I shall not be turned into a laughing stock,
or be subdued by force.
Go quickly.
As for you, you will be treated according to the rules you
follow, and you will bring the two girls before me or I will
hold you here by force.

You have acted in a way that is unworthy of your parentage,
your family and your country.

You came to Athens, a city that honours justice, that
determines nothing without recourse to the law, and you
brushed this aside, took what you wanted.

And you did this by violence, as if we in this city were without
men, or as if we were slaves.

And as if I were nothing.

And yet, Thebes didn't teach you this. Thebes does not
nurture unjust men, and Thebes would not praise you for
trying to carry off suppliants by force, suppliants who belong
to me, indeed to the gods.

I would not behave in this manner – even if I had just cause –
without permission from the ruler of the land. I would know
how a foreigner must behave among citizens. You shame a
city that does not deserve this, your own city.

You are an old man. Has the fullness of your years made you
witless?

Now, unless you want to remain a guest in this land, bring
the girls here.

CHORUS: You seem to have been bred to justice, stranger, but you
are discovered acting evilly.

KREON: I never thought this city unmanned, son of Aigeus, nor
have I acted thoughtlessly.

I only believed that the citizens of Athens would not
begrudge me my own kin and would not nurture them
against my wishes. And I knew they would not receive a
patricide – a man impure – a man who contracted a noxious
marriage – and with children. I know this country has a
council and that it forbids vagrants in the land.

You will do as you wish. I have spoken justly, but I am weak.

OEDIPUS: Arrogant and shameless. At whom do you hurl insults?
Me or yourself?
Yes, your mouth spouts my murder, my marriage, calamities
I bore unwillingly.
For a long time it pleased the gods to cherish their wrath
against my family, but take me on my own and you would not
find in me the fault which made me wrong myself and my
kin.
Tell me,
when it was prophesied to my father he would die at the
hands of his son, I wasn't born – indeed, I had not even been
seeded. What can you blame me for when I did not yet exist?
And when I was born – to misery – and I came to exchange
blows with my father and kill him, not knowing what I was
doing, or to whom,
how can you reasonably condemn this involuntary act?
As for my mother, wretch, she was your sister, but you feel no
shame in forcing me to talk of her marriage in this way. I
won't be quiet now; your mouth has soiled her.
She bore me, yes, she bore me.
I did not know it, she did not know it –
and she bore children to the child she had borne.
Disgrace.
You revile us now, but it was not my will to marry her, nor is
it my will to speak now.
I will not be marked as evil for this marriage, nor for the other
things you heap on me with your sour taunts, the death of my
father –
You tell me something in turn. If someone here, now, were to
come up to you to kill you, would you, oh very just one, try to
ascertain whether this murderer was your father, or would
you strike back promptly? I think that if you love life, you
would act immediately, not stand looking around for
justification.
The God led me into such an evil pass.
And if my father breathed again, he would not speak against
me.

CHORUS: This foreigner, lord, is deserving.
　　Events destroyed him, but he is worth helping.
THESEUS: Enough words. The captors flee and we, the wronged,
　　stand still.
　　(*To* KREON.)
　　Show me where you took these girls.
KREON: Here, you can command. At home, I shall know what to
　　do.
THESEUS: Threaten if you wish, but lead the way.
　　If your men are already on the run, mine will stop them. You
　　will not escape from here with your prize.
OEDIPUS: May you succeed, Theseus, because of your own
　　nobility and because of your just consideration towards us.

THIRD CHORUS

CHORUS

I want to be there.
Yes, there
where
Ares' bronze voice bellows – the enemy turns,
men rush, all clash.
There
along Apollo's gleaming shores,
or is it further?
Yes,
along the Eleusinian coast,
bank of mysteries,
tread of torch-lit marches
where goddesses touch mortal lips
with silence.

Yes, I see them there,
Theseus, eager for battle,
the two sisters,
and closing around them
a cry of war,
a shout of triumph.

Is it there,
or still further? Near snow-peaked Oia,
a little west, in the mountain pastures.
Horses race, foals gallop, chariots jostle.
He won't win.
No, it won't go well for Kreon –
the war rushing towards them: fearful,
the might of Theseus's men: fearful.

The expedition
gives the horses their head.
They stretch their necks, full gallop,
glitter of bridles,
young men
who worship the horse-goddess, Athene,
and the earth-hugging sea-god,
Poseidon.

Now? Not yet? Soon?
The battle –
I hope,
I believe,
I'll meet those girls soon,
hard-done by their own kin.
I prophesy a good outcome.

I'd like to be
a pigeon,
wind-tossed, fleet,
climbing high to the clouds to look
down and watch the battle,
hovering,
enjoying:
a bird's-eye view.

Zeus, Athene, Apollo – help.

Foreigner, I was no false prophet.
I see your two daughters coming this
way.

THIRD EPISODE

OEDIPUS: Where? Where? What are you saying? Where?

ANTIGONE: Father, father, oh that the gods would grant you sight of this excellent man. He brings us back to you.

OEDIPUS: Where are you? Where? Where?

ANTIGONE: Here, here, both of us.

OEDIPUS: My crutches.

ANTIGONE: Ill-fated, and ill-fated.

OEDIPUS: I have my loved ones, and I can die not totally abject now that you are here beside me. Come close to me, children, press closer, and relieve this solitary man of his fretful wanderings.

Tell me what happened.

ANTIGONE: Here is the one who saved us. Let him tell the story, father, since it was his act.

THESEUS: I am a man of deeds rather than words. Why should I boast of the victory that brought your two girls back to you? They will tell you all about it. I heard something as I was coming this way which I must put before you.

OEDIPUS: What is it, son of Aigeus?

KREON: A man, not from Thebes but still your kin, has embraced the altar of Poseidon.

OEDIPUS: Where is he from? What does he hope to achieve by this suppliant posture?

THESEUS: He asks only for a word with you, and safe-conduct on his return journey.

OEDIPUS: Who can he be?

THESEUS: Do you have any kin at Argos?

OEDIPUS: Ah – stop there.

THESEUS: What is it?

OEDIPUS: Don't ask this of me.

THESEUS: What? Say.

OEDIPUS: I know who the suppliant is.

THESEUS: Who? Would I find fault with him?

OEDIPUS: He is my son, lord, my hated son, whose words would distress me more than any other man's.

THESEUS: Can you not hear him out? Why such pain just to listen?

OEDIPUS: Abhorrent this voice, lord, to its father. Don't compel
me –

THESEUS: Are you not compelled by his status as suppliant? You
must respect the God.

ANTIGONE: Father, listen to me, even if this counsel comes from
one so young.
Let this man obey his conscience and his god.
And for our sakes too, let our brother come. He can't force
you – so what harm in hearing his words? If he means ill, his
words will betray him – it always happens.
You are his father:
Even if he had committed the worst evils against you, it
would be wrong of you to retaliate.
Let him come.
Have pity on him.
Other fathers have had criminal sons, felt the same anger, but
the pleas of their friends and kin have charmed their wrath
away.
Think of your past
your mother and father
those sufferings.
Consider carefully
and you'll see how evil anger leads to evil deeds.
Yield to us.
The granting of a just suit ought not to be withheld too long.

OEDIPUS: Your triumph, child, and for me, a wearisome defeat.
Let it be as you wish, but if he comes here, let no one have
power over my life.

THESEUS: As long as the gods look after me, you will be safe.

75

FOURTH CHORUS

CHORUS

Who asks for more of life than a moderate span of years
that man clings to madness,
manifestly stupid,
because the long days will lay out for him more grief than joy.
Joy comes hard to the man who has lived beyond what is meet.
The deliverer,
egalitarian Hades,
comes suddenly.
No wedding song or lyre there, no dance.
Silence –
Death in the end.

There is no doubt:
not to be born at all wins the day.
Or
once you've felt the warmth of the sun,
take second best and go back quickly whence you came.
Youth passes lightly
then calamities pelt down:
envy strife factions
brawls
murder
and at the end,
powerless, unsociable, repulsive old age
with all evils glued together.

It's not just me
look at this wreck
bleak north face
waves pound against him
whipped by folly
from top to bottom
wave after wave

in the rising sun
in the setting sun
in the middle ray
and in the wrap of night.

ANTIGONE: Here is the stranger, father, alone and bathed in tears.
Polyneikes.

POLYNEIKES: *Oimoi.*
What can I do? Should I lament my own troubles, sisters, or
those of my father?
In a strange land, a foreigner
shipwrecked here with the two of you.
Clad in aged and noxious filth – and his clothes in tatters.
Wild thinning hair pointing in the wind like a weathervane –
blind eyes below and a beggar's bag of rotten food.
I learn all this too late,
wretch.
And I confess I am the most evil of men in my care for you.
But next to Zeus there sits Compassion. Let her come and
stand beside you now, father.
Faults need not get worse, they can be made good.
You're silent?
Speak, father.
Something.
Will you answer nothing, but, wordless, send me away
dishonoured?
Sisters, his offspring, can you not try to stir this sullen, this
tight-lipped father?

ANTIGONE: Speak, unhappy brother. Tell him why you've come.
As your words flow, they will bring joy, or anger, or
compassion and give voice to the voiceless.

POLYNEIKES: Father, this is why I came:
I have been driven out of my country. I am the first-born. I
thought it my right to sit on your throne. But Eteokles, your
younger son, drove me out of the land.
He didn't defeat me in debate – nor in a try of strength.
No, he plotted and drew the city against me.
I suppose the curse on your house is the cause – or so I hear
from the prophets.
And so I went to the plains of Argos. There, I gained

Adrastos as father-in-law and I've gathered a powerful
army about me. Seven battalions surround the plains of
Thebes – seven battalions led by seven spears, spears
brandished by –
One: Amphiaraos, top warrior, best prophet.
Two: Tydeus – son of Oineus – from Aitolia.
Three: Eteoklos – born in Argos.
Four: Hippomedon, sent by his father, Talaos.
Five: Kapaneus – shouts he will shrink Thebes to cinders.
Six: Parthenopaios – from Arkadia – son of wild Atalanta –
rushes to join us –
Seven: Myself – your son.
If not your son, the son of an evil fate – now called your
son –
I lead this fearless army to Thebes that I might die defending
my cause – or expel those who did this –
I pray by these children, by your life, drop your anger. If
oracles are to be trusted, power will reside with those you join
– so it was said.
By the streams of our land, by the gods of our race, I beg you
to yield. We are both beggars in foreign parts, eking a living
by flattering others – we share a common doom – while he, as
king, tyrannizes over our house,
mocking us,
living the soft life, and proud.
If you stand by me, I will scatter this brother to the
winds, and I will establish us both.
If you want these things, they will be possible, but
without you, I can do nothing.
Without you, I won't even return alive –
CHORUS: Speak, Oedipus, for the sake of Theseus, speak as you
    see fit before you send him away.
OEDIPUS: You, evil one, when you had the throne and sceptre,
    you drove me out, you made me cityless.
    Then you were happy to see me in these clothes, which now
    make you weep – now that your brother has driven you out.
    You made your own father an exile, a man without a city.

No time for me to weep, I must bear these things out,
remembering that my murderer is you.
Because of you I wander, because of you I grovel each day for
my food.
And if I had not produced these two children, my nurses,
dear nurturers, I would not be alive now, for all your
concern.
Now these girls keep me fed.
These girls are men, not women.
Companions in pain.
You were sired by someone else, not me.
But fate does not look on you now as it will soon if and when
armies march towards Thebes.
For you will never succeed in bringing down that city. You
will fall, covered in the pollution of kindred blood, and your
brother the same. Those are the curses I called down on you
before and now I ask these to be my allies so that you may
learn to respect your progenitor and not to dishonour him –
him, the blind father who begot you. These girls did not do
this.
And my curses hold more power than any supplication, any
throne.
You, go now, hated, unfathered – you, most evil of evil, and
take with you these curses.
I call forth this: you are never to triumph over your native
land in war
nor ever to return to the plains of Argos
but to die at the hands of your kin and to kill the one who
drove you out –
such are my prayers.
And I call upon the abhorred darkness of Hades
Father of Tartaros
your true father
to take you to another home.
I call on the spirits of this place
and I call on Ares the destroyer, who has forged this terrible
hatred between you and your brother.

You've heard these things.
Go now, and tell the Thebans and your own allies what
honours Oedipus has chosen to distribute among his sons.
CHORUS: Polyneikes, I had no joy in your coming, and now you
must go back quickly.
POLYNEIKES: *Oimoi.*
Woe to my journey, my ill-success, and woe to my friends.
Sisters, you've heard the harsh prayers of my father, don't
you –
if his curses are fulfilled –
don't, by the gods, if you ever return home,
don't let me be dishonoured in death, but bury me in a tomb
– with due funeral honours.
ANTIGONE: Polyneikes, I implore you to listen to me.
POLYNEIKES: Loved sister, what is it? Say.
ANTIGONE: Turn back the armies of Argos. Why destroy yourself
and the city?
POLYNEIKES: That is not possible. How can I ever lead if I run
now?
ANTIGONE: Why such anger, child? What gain in destroying your
own city?
POLYNEIKES: Shame in being an exile. Laughed at by a younger
brother.
ANTIGONE: Don't you see how you fulfil his prophecies,
his cry that you will both die at each other's hands?
POLYNEIKES: Don't stop me.
I have chosen a bad road –
Unlucky because of my father and his avenging spirits.
ANTIGONE: Misery.
POLYNEIKES: Don't weep for me.
ANTIGONE: Who would not weep seeing you march towards
Hades, brother?
POLYNEIKES: This lies with destiny – if I must die, I will die.
(*Exits.*)
CHORUS: New things come to me, and more new things.
Evil and oppressive; they come from the foreigner. And now
the heavens crack –

81

thunder –
Listen to the heavens. Oh Zeus.

OEDIPUS: The winged thunder of Zeus will lead me to Death.
Send for Theseus, don't delay.

CHORUS: Bigger.
Listen:
noise crashing down.
My hair stands on end.
Fear.
Oh great heavens. Oh Zeus.

OEDIPUS: Is he coming? Will he find me still breathing and of
sound mind?

THESEUS: What is it, child of Laios, what new thing?

OEDIPUS: The sinking of the scale. My life dips down. I want
to die without failing in my promise to you and to the
city.

THESEUS: Tell me what must be done.

OEDIPUS: I will teach you, child of Aigeus, what
will never suffer of decay or of old age.
I myself will lead you to the place – without a guide – where I
must die.
And you must never tell of this to any man.
When you come to the place alone, you will understand
these mysteries. I cannot say anything to these people, not
even to my children, however much I love them.
You must guard this secret alone, and when you are old, tell
it only to your heir, and he to his.
And in this way you will live unconquered by the
Thebans.
Now: to the place.
The summons of the God drives me forward.
Children, follow me – I am your guide now.
Come – don't touch me –
I will find the sacred tomb alone.
This way – here – this way – come.
Hermes leads, and the goddess of the dead.
Light – darkness for me – clings to my body for the last time.

Now, hidden, alone with Hades,
my life
closes.
And you, beloved strangers, may you and your land be
blessed. Remember me always, for your own good fortune.

FIFTH CHORUS

CHORUS

Queens of the deep-delved earth
and you,
beast, who –
so they say from long ago –
lies by those guest-worn gates,
unconquerable watcher of Hades,
whimpering from the deep caves,
and you, child of Earth and Tartaros,
I pray that the foreigner departing for
the lower levels of the dead
find his path clear.

FIFTH EPISODE

MESSENGER: Citizens, let me say very briefly that Oedipus is dead.
How it happened, that is another story –

CHORUS: The unhappy man is gone?

MESSENGER: Yes, be sure of that.

CHORUS: How? Ordained by God? Without pain?

MESSENGER: That you may wonder at. You know how he left –
you were here – you saw: guided by no friend, he led us.
When he came to the bronze steps which fix the earth's deep
roots, he stopped on one of the many branching paths, near
that hollow basin, there where Theseus and Perithous had a
covenant – where their tokens of faith lie.
He stood between the Thorikian stone and the hollow pear
tree and then he sat on the marble tomb.
He loosened his filthy clothes and he told his children to
bring him fresh water so that he might drink and pour
libations.
And the two went to the hill of evergreen Demeter – the hill
you see – and quickly brought fresh water to their father, and
they decked him out in the proper manner, and they bathed
him.
When all was done, everything he'd ordered
then thunder from Zeus of the dark Earth –
and the girls trembled as they heard
and fell to the knees of their father and beat their chests
and again
and wailed
and wailed loudly
and hearing this sudden, this bitter cry
he holds them in his hands and says:
Children
Your father is no more for you today.
Everything of mine has died and you will no longer be bound
to your toilsome nurturing – bitter and harsh task, I know,
children. Yet one word will lighten these labours.
This:

85

no man loved you as much as I.
Now, for the rest of your lives, no more.
They clung, they wept, all three.
When the laments quieted
and the shouts flaked
a silence
and then a voice
to make the hair stand on end.
And the god called him, called him again, in many ways.
This man, this man Oedipus, why delay?
You've stayed too long.
He understood the God's call.
He called Theseus to him.
He said:
Give your hand to my children as a pledge of loyalty and you,
children, give your hands to this man.
Promise never to abandon these girls and to fulfil all your
good intentions towards them.
Theseus promised,
noble and dry-eyed,
restrained.
Oedipus stretches his blind hands to his children,
says:
You must endure, be noble.
Leave this place and never ask to see what you must not, nor
to hear what it is not right to hear.
Go quickly
let Theseus stand by and understand what is taking place.
We all heard
we all filed away
all in tears
followed the girls away.
But after we'd gone, we soon looked back
and we saw the man was not there.
Only the king himself, shielding his eyes as if something
terrible had appeared,
something not to be seen.

Then we saw him prostrate himself to the ground and call to
the earth and to the gods above in one prayer.

How Oedipus died, no mortal knows, save Theseus.

No thunderbolt

no whirlwind from the sea.

Perhaps a messenger from the gods.

Perhaps the earth opened in love,

kindly opened for him to go without pain.

He went without cries, or sickness or suffering, no,

for a mortal: wonderful.

And if I seem to speak without sense, what can I do?

Some people will call me insane:

let them.

CHORUS: Where are the girls?

MESSENGER: Not far. You can hear them.

ANTIGONE: *Aiai.*

    Feu.

Mourn now the curse on this blood come to us from our
father

Aiai, aiai, aiai, aiai. Ill-fated two

Where can we go?

ISMENE: Death, join me to my father.

The life I have to live is no life.

CHORUS: Children, excellent sisters, you've endured well the
fortunes sent by God.

Don't be fired now by too much grief.

ANTIGONE: That which ought not to have been loved was loved
when I had him in my hands.

Father, friend, now clothed in the dark of death.

Even there we will love you.

CHORUS: His end was happy, ease your pain –

ANTIGONE: Sister, let's run back.

ISMENE: What?

ANTIGONE: I must go.

ISMENE: Where?

ANTIGONE: To the dark-earthed hearth.

ISMENE: Whose?

ANTIGONE: Father
Ah, misfortune –
ISMENE: It's not allowed. Don't you see?
ANTIGONE: Why rebuke me?
ISMENE: He died with
no tomb
and far from all.
ANTIGONE: Take me there. My death over his.
ISMENE: *Aiai.*
Misery.
How am I to drag out my life alone, abandoned, always
unhappy, without a friend, without help? Where am I to
spend my life?
THESEUS: Enough tears, children.
Where the grace of primeval power is
manifest, it is not necessary to mourn:
there lies nemesis; beware divine anger.
ANTIGONE: Son of Aigeus, we beg you –
THESEUS: What is your request, children?
ANTIGONE: We wish to see our father's tomb.
THESEUS: It is not allowed.
ANTIGONE: What are you saying?
THESEUS: He told me no one should go near the place nor speak
about it. If I did these things, I would hold the country safe.
Pledges heard by the gods and by divine Oath, the servant of
Zeus.
ANTIGONE: If this was his purpose, it must suffice.
And now, send us to ancient Thebes that we might stop the
bloodshed between our brothers.
THESEUS: I will do that and anything else. And I will never grow
weary of this task, for the sake of the man below ground, who
passed away from us not long ago.
CHORUS: Cease to lament, cause no disturbance. All is in order
and under control.

ANTIGONE

PROLOGUE

Thebes.

ANTIGONE: My own sister, dear sister, Ismene.
Tell me this: are there any evils coming from Oedipus that
Zeus does not fulfil through us – the two still living?
Pain, ruin, shame
all of these
I see in your evils and mine.
And now what is this proclamation the general has made to
all of Thebes?
Have you heard anything? Are you aware that evils
appropriate for our enemies are to be endured by our loved
ones?

ISMENE: I have no word, Antigone, concerning loved ones.
Nothing sweet, nothing bitter, has come my way since we two
were bereft of our two brothers – one day's double blow of a
double death. And with the departure of the armies from
Argos last night, I do not know whether to feel more
fortunate or more distressed.

ANTIGONE: I know –
And I've brought you outside the gates of the house so that
you alone can hear.

ISMENE: What is it? You're troubled – brooding over some
story.

ANTIGONE: We have two brothers. Hasn't Kreon honoured one
with a tomb and shamed the other?
Eteokles, they say, has been buried, with due observance of
justice and custom, under the ground, to be honoured among
the dead.
As for Polyneikes, they say it is forbidden by decree to bury
him, or mourn him, but he is to be left unwept, unburied, a
sweet morsel for the birds as they look down – their treasure
store of tasty meat.
That is the good Kreon's proclamation to you and to me –

yes, to me – and he is coming here to make this clear to those
who may still not know.

And this is no small matter.

Whoever does these things anyway will be stoned in front of
the people of the city. That's how it is for you as well and you
will soon show whether you are well born or the bad shoot of
good stock.

ISMENE: If these things are so, my poor sister, what can I do? Not
do?

ANTIGONE: Think if you will share in the work, the act.

ISMENE: Share in what? What do you mean?

ANTIGONE: Will you help this hand to lift the dead?

ISMENE: You are thinking of burying him – and this has been
forbidden?

ANTIGONE: He is my own brother, and yours too, even if you do
not wish it. I will not be known as the one who betrayed him.

ISMENE: Such purpose – and Kreon has forbidden it.

ANTIGONE: Not for him to keep me from my own.

ISMENE: *Oimoi.*

Think,
sister
how our father died –
hated, in shame,
shunned,
uncovering himself his own guilt and striking his two eyes
with his own hands. And then the mother, wife, double
name, mangling her life in that tangle of ropes.

And finally, our two brothers, in one day each miserably
slaying the other, trapped in a shared fate wreaked by their
own hands.

We are the two left behind. Alone. We too will die most
miserably if we violate the decree and defy the power of the
tyrant.

We must remember we are born women and are not meant to
do battle against men.

And then that we are ruled by those who are the stronger and
we must obey this and things even more painful.

And so I beg forgiveness of those below, I am compelled: I
have to obey those in power.

There is no sense in the excessive gesture.

ANTIGONE: I won't urge you any more – no, even if you changed
and wanted to do it – you would no longer be welcome.

Think as you will.

I will bury him.

And I will die well doing this.

I will lie with him I love, my friend, my kin – guilty, yes, but
of a holy crime.

I believe I owe more of my time to pleasing the dead below
than those here: for there, I shall lie for ever.

Think as you will, but you will be guilty of dishonouring the
gods.

ISMENE: I am not doing them a dishonour.

I cannot act against the will of the city.

ANTIGONE: Such is your excuse.

I will go and raise a tomb for my beloved brother.

ISMENE: Hard-suffering, I fear for you.

ANTIGONE: Don't fear for me; straighten out your own destiny.

ISMENE: At least keep this plan to yourself. I will do the same.

ANTIGONE: Announce it. I will hate you more if you remain silent
and you don't proclaim this to everyone.

ISMENE: You have a hot spirit for chill acts.

ANTIGONE: I know I am giving satisfaction to those I owe it to.

ISMENE: If you have that power. But you want the impossible.

ANTIGONE: And so – when I have no more strength, I shall stop.

ISMENE: For a start, it is not fitting to pursue the impossible.

ANTIGONE: If you keep saying these things, you will incur not only
my own hatred but that of the dead as well; you will be
exposed as their enemy.

Let me suffer my own folly in this terrible deed. I would
suffer more if I did not come to a good death.

ISMENE: Go, if it seems right to you.

And know this: you go senselessly, but rightly loved by your
loved ones.

FIRST CHORUS

CHORUS

Sun ray
most beautiful
ever seen in Thebes – Thebes of the seven gates
at last you come to us
golden eye of day
opening over the streams of Dirke.
And then
the army from Argos, the army of white shields
saw you and
already routed, fled fast, sped on,
bridles aglint in the new day.

This army
because of Polyneikes
Polyneikes and his dubious and many claims
came clashing and clanging over our land
covering our earth:
a long eagle-wing, white as snow
mottled plumage of white weapons and horsehair helmets
hovering
over our roofs.
No movement,
gaping mouth,
widening circle
around our gates, teeth of bloody spears
hungry
then:
left.
No blood filling its cheeks.
No crowns of towers
feeding the fire of its torches.
No, the din of Ares followed close on the army's back.
They could not conquer the dragon's

kin – the sons of Thebes.

Zeus hates, utterly hates, the boasts of
a flat and flatulent tongue.
He watches him – haughty glint and clang of gold,
about to open his mouth to shout victory
standing there on our very ramparts.
Zeus watches and then hurls him down
with a lightning streak.
He swings in the air, he falls, he crashes.
The echo:
thump
crack
twangs through ground.
The one who attacked, mad with fire,
blowing his hateful winds on Thebes.
It did not go his way at all
and great Ares distributed other fates to the others.
They all splintered against his might.
Ares, our ally, worked hard.

Seven captains stand before seven gates
equal against equal
leave behind their offerings to Zeus
Zeus who helps in war.

But two
loathsome and wretched
born of the same father, the same mother
two brothers brandish two spears and
the two split one death.

Victory, great named victory, has come –
radiant, gracious – to Thebes, full of joy
Thebes, covered in chariots.
So now:
war is over, forget it;

let us go to the temples of the gods
and dance through the night
Bakchos in the lead
threading through, treading on, rattling
the soil of Thebes.

FIRST EPISODE

CHORUS: Here comes the king of this country, Kreon son of
Menoikeus. The new ruler, according to the recent fortunes
bestowed by the gods. What idea does he ponder as he
approaches? Why has he summoned us here? Why has he
convoked this special meeting of elders?

KREON: Citizens. Our affairs, lately tossed into such disarray, have
once again been brought to order by the gods.

I sent messengers to call on you separately because I know
that you revere the power and the throne of Laios.

And that when Oedipus ruled the city and later died, you
remained concerned for his sons.

And now they – Eteokles and Polyneikes – have been struck
down in one day by a double fate, each striking and each
struck by murder, each stained by the death of his kin.

And because of my kinship with the dead I now hold the
power and the throne.

A man's soul, spirit, judgement, will not be known until he
has been seen to exercise power and the rule of law. And it
seems to me that anyone who, while guiding the city, does
not cling to the best policies but keeps his tongue under
guard – out of some fear – this man I hold and have always
held to be the worst of men.

As for anyone who holds his own kin more important than his
own country, I call that man beneath contempt. I – let Zeus
know this, who sees everything always – I would not remain
silent if I saw ruin rather than prosperity come towards my
city. And I would never call a man hostile to this land my
friend.

Because I know this:

The city is our ship of safety and only when she sails a straight
course can we make the friends we should.

And it is with these rules that I will increase the power of this
city.

I have now decreed kindred rules regarding the sons of
Oedipus.

First Eteokles:
He died fighting for our city, he was our champion, most
noble in battle.
Eteokles will be buried in a grave and be given all due rites
proper to the best of those who have fallen.
Second, his brother – I mean Polyneikes. He returned from
exile to his country, and to his gods,
and he wanted to burn it down, destroy it by fire from top to
bottom.
He wanted to drink the blood of kinsmen and take the rest
away as slaves.
For that man, this has been proclaimed:
He is to remain unburied, uncleansed by funeral rites and
unlamented,
a corpse eaten by birds and dogs: a mangling for all to see.
Such is my purpose.
Never will I decree that evil men shall be honoured instead of
the just. But the man who is well disposed to the city, be he
dead or alive, that man I shall honour.

CHORUS: It lies in your pleasure, Kreon, to decide the fate of
those well disposed and ill disposed to our city. And you
can apply whatever law you wish over the dead and over us,
the living.

KREON: See then that no one breaks the edict.

CHORUS: Trust this task to a younger man.

KREON: There are already guardians for the corpse.

CHORUS: What other orders could you have for us?

KREON: Not to side with those who disobey.

CHORUS: No one is so foolish as to wish for death.

KREON: Yes, that is the price to pay.
But the hope of profit has killed many a man.

GUARD: Lord.
I will not say I have come breathless from rushing here.
Or indeed that I have been light on my feet.
No. I stopped many times to take thought.
And many times I turned around to go back where I came
from.

For my soul had many things to say as it talked to me:
Unhappy one, why are you going there? You'll pay a heavy
price for it. Most unhappy and reckless one, look: now you're
stopping again.
And what if Kreon hears these things from someone else,
won't you suffer for that as well?
Turning these things around in my mind all the time I
hurried and completed my journey slowly. In such a way a
short road can become a long one.
And so at least, anyway, coming here won out. Here I am.
And even if I have nothing to say I will speak nevertheless.
For I've grasped one hope firmly, which is not to suffer
anything except that which is my destined allotment.

KREON: What's the cause of such despondency?

GUARD: First I want to tell you all about myself'
I did not do the deed, I did not see who did it, so it wouldn't
be justice for me to come to harm.

KREON: Your words are well aimed. You fence yourself off from
this deed. Clearly you have something new to reveal.

GUARD: Yes, but terrible things make one terribly afraid.

KREON: Will you not speak and release us of your presence?

GUARD: Yes indeed, I'll tell you.
The corpse: someone has given it burial and gone away – has
sprinkled dry dust on the body, having performed the
necessary pious rites.

KREON: What are you saying?
What man has had the recklessness, the boldness, to do this?

GUARD: I don't know. There was no evidence of the work of a
pick-axe or hoe. The ground was hard, dry and unbroken; no
track of wheels.
The doer left without a sign.
And when the first watchman showed it to us, we were all
deeply distressed. For the body was covered, but not buried;
a light dust covered him, as if someone wished to escape from
the guilt of an unburied corpse.
No signs either of a wild animal, or a dog who came near him
or tore at him.

99

And now, loud arguments started rising among us.
Guard questioning guard – and it would have come to blows.
No one could stop it – we were all guilty, but not one more
guilty than the other.
And we all claimed we knew nothing of the deed.
And there we were, each ready to hold red-hot iron in his
hands, to crawl through fire, to swear by the gods he didn't
do it and didn't know who did, and never had anything to do
with the planning of it.
Finally someone spoke and made us drop our heads with fear
by suggesting this:
and we couldn't oppose him, but we couldn't accept what
would happen to us if we did as he said.
His advice was that this deed would have to be reported to
you and not covered up. That's what finally was decided and
it was my bad destiny to have the lot fall to me – to do this
good thing.
So here I am: unwilling and unwelcome, I know that much.
For no one loves the messenger who brings bad news.

CHORUS: Lord, I have been thinking that this might well be the
work of the gods.

KREON: Stop before your words fill me with anger and you
yourselves are discovered to be not only old but mindless. It
is intolerable for you to say that the gods would have any
intentions regarding this corpse. Are you saying they wanted
to cover him with the highest honours due a benefactor?
When he came to burn down the pillars of their temples and
their offerings? When he came to burn their land and scatter
their laws? Is that it? The gods honour evil men now, do
they?
It is not so.
From the moment the edict was proclaimed, there were men
in this city who were whispering against me, who were tossing
their heads defiantly, instead of submitting their necks to the
yoke, as they should in justice – honouring me. And I know, I
have no doubt, that it was these men who induced the guards
to do this – in return for payment.

For there has never grown among men a more evil currency than money.

It lays cities to waste, drives men from their homes.

It teaches and twists good minds to shameful deeds.

It shows men how to practise every villainy, and how to embrace impiety.

However, all those who hired themselves out for this deed have made certain they will sooner or later find their punishment.

And as I still revere Zeus, know this well –

Yes, I say this to you on oath: if you do not find the perpetrator of this burial – produce him before my very eyes – you will have worse than death coming to you: you will hang alive until you confess your crime –

That way you will know in future where to look for profit and that it is best not to seek gain wherever it is offered. And you will see that most men have found ruin rather than safety in dishonest gain.

GUARD: Will you allow me to speak? Or should I turn around and go away?

KREON: Don't you know how offensive your words are?

GUARD: Do they sting your ears or your soul?

KREON: Why are you interested in the anatomy of my pain?

GUARD: The doer distresses your mind, but I your ears.

KREON: You are nothing but a babbler.

GUARD: At least I never did the deed.

KREON: You did more; you sold your soul for money.

GUARD: *Feu.*

It's terrible when the one who makes decisions makes the wrong ones.

KREON: If you don't produce the culprit, you will see that paltry gains produce terrible sufferings.

GUARD: I certainly hope he'll be found.

Whether he is caught or not – and chance will decide that one – you can be sure of not seeing me here again.

I'm still alive, against all hope and expectation, and I owe great thanks to the gods.

SECOND CHORUS

CHORUS

Wonder
at many things
But wonder most
at this thing:
Man
who
crosses the speckled sea
across winter storms
past the high rise of gaping
waves,
and
criss-crosses the land
wearing away, scratching
the immortal, immutable
goddess earth
as he turns up the soil
year after year
with the mule-drawn plough.

He has found a way
to weave the different nets
that ensnare giddy birds
trap the wild species of the plains
and catch the dwellers of the sea.
Ingenious man,
who's found devices
to master the mountain –
hopping goat –
to tame the horse
(halter round its shaggy neck)
the massive bull.

*Polla ta deina kouden anthropou
deinoteron pelei
touto kai poliou peran pontou
cheimerio
noto
chorei perbruchioisin peroon hup
oidmasin.*

*theon te tan hupertatan Gan
aphthiton, akamatan apotruetai
illomenon arotron etos eis etos
hippeio genei poleuon.*

He taught himself speech   *kai phthegma kai anemoen*
thought light as wind   *phronema kai astunomous orgas*
the passions that raise cities   *edidaxato*
and   *kai dusaulon*
how to escape the bitter shafts   *pagon hupaithreia kai dusombra*
   of rain   *pheugein*
the frost   *ebele*
the wrath of the open sky.   *pantoporos aporos ep ouden*
Nothing stops him: *erchetai*
he finds his way through   *to mellon. Haida monon pheuxin*
   everything.   *ouk*
From death alone he sees no   *expaxetai*
   way out,   *noson d'amechanon fugas*
even though   *xumpephrastai*
he discovers routes through stubborn diseases.

Subtle beyond conceit
this inventive skill
with which he moves
sometimes to evil and sometimes to good.
When he respects the laws of his land
and keeps his oath to the gods' justice
then his city rises high.
But
the one who is reckless
ignoble
that man is city-less
a nomad – nothing.
Let him not come to my hearth
or near my thoughts
if that's the way he's going.

SECOND EPISODE

CHORUS: Oh gods, what marvel do you set before us now?
    How can I deny, when I can see it so clearly, that this is the child Antigone?
    Sorry child of the sorry Oedipus.
    What's this? Surely it isn't you they've caught disobeying the laws of the king? It isn't you they are bringing here, lost to all sense?

GUARD: Here is the one who has done the deed.
    We caught her in the act of burial.
    Where is Kreon?

CHORUS: He's coming back from his house just as we need him.

KREON: What is it? Why is my arrival so opportune?

GUARD: Lord, no mortal should ever take an oath.
    For second thoughts soon prove first thoughts false.
    I vowed I would only ever come here again very very slowly, because I'd been sorely afflicted by your threats before –
    However, there is no greater pleasure than a joy that has not even been prayed for. And so here I am,
    unfaithful to my oath, but: bringing the girl.
    She was caught performing due rites of burial.
    No need to draw lots this time:
    this is my godsend, not another's.
    And now, lord, do as you wish with this girl I have caught, questions and examine her. I have the right to be free, and released from these evils.

KREON: This girl you bring, how did you take her? Where?

GUARD: She was burying that man. That's it.

KREON: Do you hear what you are saying? Is what you are saying accurate?

GUARD: I saw her burying the corpse, the one forbidden. Isn't what I'm saying clear and intelligible?

KREON: How was she seen? How was she caught?

GUARD: It happened this way:
    When we had come to that place, with your dreadful threats hanging over us, we swept away all the dust that covered the

104

body, and left it bare, putrid. We took shelter in the hills,
upwind, so that the smell wouldn't hit us.
Every man was awake, and made sure he kept his
companions awake with a lot of bad language, just in case
anyone neglected his work.
Time passed.
The sun's bright disk climbed midway up the sky.
Pelted down its heat.
And then –
on a sudden –
a whirlwind lifts a storm of dust from the earth – a blur in the
heavens –
The dust fills the plain, mangles the leaves in the woods and
fills the air with its wreckage.
We keep our eyes shut –
Wait patiently for the god's scourge to pass.
It takes a long time.
For it to go away.
Then was the girl seen.
She lamented with the bitter cry of a bird
who discovers an empty nest, the bed stripped of nestlings.
Just so, when she sees the body stripped of dust, she howls,
she wails and calls down evil curses on those who have done
this.
And at once, she carries the dry, the thirsty dust in her
hands. And from a finely wrought bronze pitcher, which she
raises high, she wreaths the corpse with a triple libation.
When we see this, we pounce and catch her – she is not
panicked at all. And we question her thoroughly about her
deeds, what she did before and what she's doing now.
She denies nothing.
Now this was sweet to me but also painful.
It's a sweet thing to have escaped from trouble oneself. But
to bring friends into trouble, that is painful. But it's only
natural I should find all that less important than my own
safety.

KREON: And you

bending your head to the ground, speak:

Do you deny this in any way or do you admit to doing it?

ANTIGONE: I admit to doing it and I in no way deny it.

KREON: (*To* GUARD) Take yourself where you please, you're free of a serious charge.

But you, tell me this, concisely: did you know there was a proclamation forbidding these things?

ANTIGONE: I knew. How could I not? It was made public.

KREON: And you still had the effrontery to transgress the laws?

ANTIGONE: Yes, why not? It was not Zeus who made this proclamation.

Nor did Justice, which lives with the gods below, prescribe the observance of such laws to men.

And I did not suppose that your proclamations were so strong, that a mortal could thereby overrule the unwritten, the immutable laws of the gods.

For these are not of yesterday, not of today, but now and for ever. And no one knows whence they first arose.

I do not intend to pay the price to the gods for breaking these, because I fear one man's will.

I knew I would die. What of it?

Even if you had not proclaimed this.

If I am to die before my time I count that a gain. When anyone lives, as I do, surrounded by evils, how can such a person find anything but gain in death?

If, then, this fate is to strike me, it causes me little pain, but –

If the dead son of my mother and of my father were to remain unburied, a prey to the dogs, then I would indeed be in pain

And I suppose I could say that if my deeds seem stupid to you, perhaps it is because they are stupidly judged.

CHORUS: Fierce child of a fierce father: she will not bend in adversity.

KREON: You should know that it is the hardest wills that collapse most easily. And that the hardest iron tempered in the hottest fire is most easily shattered. I have seen the lightest of

bits tame the most spirited horses.
One should not be so high-minded when one is the slave of
others.
This girl has already shown hubris when she knowingly
transgressed the laws laid down. And she goes further, more
hubris, double hubris, when she boasts of what she's done
and makes a mockery of us.
And now:
I am no longer a man,
she is the man
if she is to be credited with the power to do such things and
go unpunished.
No: even if she is my sister's child nearer to me in blood than
any other of my house and hearth – this hearth protected by
Zeus –
even then
she and her kin will not escape a dire fate.
I charge the other one as well with an equal share in planning
this tomb. Call her now.
I saw her inside, raving and out of her mind. The mind of
those planning crooked things in the dark is likely to convict
itself ahead of the deed.
I hate this.
And I hate it even more when someone caught in the act of
evil wants to turn it into something beautiful.

ANTIGONE: Do you want anything more than to convict me and
put me to death?

KREON: No. Nothing. Having that I have everything.

ANTIGONE: Why delay? Your words give me no pleasure – may
they never do so. And I am sure that anything I say will only
displease you.
And yet, how could I win a more glorious fame than by
placing my own brother in a grave?
And these people here would all confess their pleasure, if fear
hadn't shut down their mouths.
Tyranny has many ways of prospering, since it can do and say
what it wills.

KREON: You're the only Theban to see it that way.

ANTIGONE: They see it, but draw in their tongues.

KREON: Aren't you ashamed to think so differently from these people?

ANTIGONE: There is no shame in respecting those from the same womb.

KREON: Wasn't it a blood brother who died on the opposite side?

ANTIGONE: Blood brother of the same mother and of the same father.

KREON: Your are impious to him when you so honour the other.

ANTIGONE: The dead one would not give such evidence.

KREON: He would if you honour him no better than you honour the impious one.

ANTIGONE: It was not a slave who died, but a brother.

KREON: Destroying this land. The other defended it.

ANTIGONE: None the less, Hades demands these observances.

KREON: But not for the good man to receive the same as the evil one.

ANTIGONE: Who knows that these things seem holy to those below?

KREON: Never is an enemy
even in death
a friend.

ANTIGONE: It is not my nature to join in enmity, but in love.

KREON: Join them below, then, if you must love them so, these loved ones.
As long as I live, no woman shall rule me.

CHORUS: There is Ismene, in front of the gates. Tears of a loving sister pouring down. Cloud over her brow. Shadows mar her flushed face. Cheeks drenched.

KREON: You –
Shake in my house, surreptitiously draining my blood.
I never knew I was raising two agencies of ruin, two rebels to my power.
Tell me this: will you admit you had a share in this burial or will you deny all knowledge if it?

ISMENE: I did the deed, if she agrees with me. I partook in it –

and I share the guilt.

ANTIGONE: No. Justice will not allow you that. You did not wish for it and I did not give you a share of it.

ISMENE: You're beset with evils; I am not ashamed to be your companion in suffering.

ANTIGONE: Hades and the dead below are the chronicles of this deed. I cannot love a friend who is a friend in words only.

ISMENE: Don't, sister, turn away and reject me now. Don't stop me from dying with you. Let me give due honour to the dead.

ANTIGONE: You cannot share my death. Don't lay claim to deeds you didn't even come close to. My own death is sufficient.

ISMENE: How can I love a life that is deprived of you?

ANTIGONE: Ask Kreon. Your care is for him now.

ISMENE: Why distress me so when it doesn't help you?

ANTIGONE: I don't want to revile you – it's painful for me . . .

ISMENE: How can I help?

ANTIGONE: Save yourself. I don't resent your escape.

ISMENE: *Oimoi talaina.*

I'm to miss out on your fate.

ANTIGONE: You choose to live, I to die.

ISMENE: I warned you. I spoke.

ANTIGONE: Some will say you chose well, some will say I did.

ISMENE: We have an equal share in failure.

ANTIGONE: Courage.

You live.

I have given my life to death, so that I might care for the dead.

KREON: I'd say of these two children that one has recently lost her mind and the other seems to have been born without any mind at all.

ISMENE: The mind given to us by nature will not hold, lord, when it goes through so many evil fortunes. It must give way.

KREON: Yours certainly did when you chose to go along with evil.

ISMENE: What life is left for me, without her?

KREON: Don't speak of 'her'. She is no more.

ISMENE: You'll also kill the marriage of your own son?

KREON: He'll find others to produce his children.

ISMENE: There was never a more fitting marriage – for him or for her.

KREON: I'd hate an evil wife for my son.

ISMENE: Sweet Haimon, your father deprives you of your rights.

KREON: I've had enough of you and your marriages.

CHORUS: Will you rob your son of this woman?

KREON: It is Death's nature to put an end to marriage.

CHORUS: The decision seems to have been made: she will die.

KREON: So it seems to you, and to me as well.
  No more delays.
  Call the slaves to take these women inside.
  These women must no longer be allowed to roam freely.
  Even the bold try to flee when they see Death's shadow fall across their life.

THIRD CHORUS

Fortunate the one
who goes through life
with no taste of trouble.

Once
a seismic god
shakes a house in his fist,
then
no warp, coil, no twist of
ruin   *ATE*
will go missing.
That is
ate,
weaving through the generations.
You know the sea:
In a northern storm, straight from
Thrace,
how it swells over the gloomy deep
churns black sand from the sea bed.
You've heard the cliffs
moan as winds pound them
and again.
You've seen the cliff face crack.

See how far back they go
these ancient sorrows
of the Labdakid house.
Sorrows of the living
pile on sorrows of the dead.
The new generation does not release
the old one
no
a god comes crashing through.

No ease, ever.
Remember:
there was hope.
a light spread over the house of
Oedipus,
a new shoot, lustrous.
What happened next?
Look:
the blood-red cleaver of some nether
god
cuts her down
chops
her words without sense
and the fury of her mind.

You
Zeus
have a power
a man may cross
but not hold back.
Not even that hungry hunter,
Sleep
nor
the unwearied months
bridle it. You rule
supreme – free of time –
over the glinting marble of Olympus.

And always, now and for ever and ever,
this law holds:
excess does not enter a mortal life
without bringing ruin –   *ATE*
Wayward hope may console some
but for others: delusion.
The cheat of giddy desires
seeps into the ignorant man
until flames singe his foot.

These words were wisely said:
Evil will seem good
to the man whose mind a god leads
to ruin.   *ATE*
He'll fare well for a day,
but then: Wreckage.   *ATE, ATE, ATE*

THIRD EPISODE

CHORUS: Here comes Haimon, your last and youngest son. Is he
grieving over Antigone's fate? In agony at being cheated of his
marriage?

KREON: No need of a prophet to answer that. Child:
You've heard of the final decision concerning your bride.
Have you come raving against your father?
Or do we remain kin and friends, whatever happens?

HAIMON: Father, I am yours.
Your good judgements can guide me aright, and these I
intend to follow.
No marriage could seem as worthwhile to me as being nobly
guided by you.

KREON: Indeed, son, keep this resolve in your heart and accept all
of your father's judgements.
Men pray for no more than this: to produce obedient sons
and have them at home –
So that these may requite evil with evil when enemies are at
the gates; and offer as much honour to the friend as does the
father.
But when a man has begotten unhelpful children, it can be
said he has produced nothing but pain for himself – and laid
himself open to the derision of his enemies.
And so, child, don't now, for the sake of the pleasure that
comes from a woman, take leave of your senses. You know
than an evil woman in one's house, in one's bed, soon
becomes a dank object of embrace.
What sore festers with more virulence than an evil friend?
And so, spit her out, this enemy, let her drop down to Hades
and find herself a husband there.
I have caught her, alone of all the citizens, in open
disobedience and I will not prove myself a liar to the city, no,
I will kill her.
Let her sing all her prayers to the god of kinship – yes, to
Zeus –
If I nourish disorder amongst my own, what will I be

114

encouraging outside?

I know that the man who is effective in his own household will appear just to the city.

Whoever transgresses and does violence to the laws, whoever believes they can order around someone in power, that person must not expect to win my praise.

For the one appointed by the city must be obeyed in small matters, in just ones and in their opposite.

I believe that the man who is content to be ruled is capable of ruling well himself.

Anarchy is the worst of evils.

It wrecks cities, ravages households. It helps the enemy to rout one's allies: whereas order and obedience of the rules saves many lives.

Because of this, we must always defend the decisions of those who are responsible for order and in no way make ourselves inferior to women.

If one must fall, let it be at the hands of a man, but never so as to be perceived as beneath women.

CHORUS: It seems to us – unless we are deceived by old age – that your words are very sensible.

HAIMON: Father, the mind is the greatest gift the gods have produced for men.

And I myself would never, indeed could never, say whether your words are right or not.

However, my natural position makes me listen to everything that other men say – what they object to, what they find fault with.

This because the common man would find your frown too terrifying were he to say something which displeased you.

It is for me to hear these things under the cover of darkness. And in this city, I hear:

laments for this girl, who does not deserve this harm, how she is dying, when she should not, this woman who deserves glory and fame –

this woman who, when her brother fell to the slaughter, would not allow the dogs to gnaw at him nor the birds to pick

at his body. Ought she not to be crowned with honours?
These are the words spreading noiselessly over the city.
There is no possession I value more, father, than your own
prosperity. Indeed, there is no greater prize for children than
a father who is flourishing in glory.
But listen:
Don't fix in yourself only one kind of disposition so that you
feel that only what you say is right – nothing else.
Those who think that they alone have judgement, that they
alone have speech, a soul, and that no one else does, those
people, when they are opened up, are often found to be
empty.
There is nothing shameful when a man, even a wise man,
learns something. No one ought to be stretched too taut.
Look at the trees near the winter torrents, how they bend to
the wind and so preserve their branches, whereas those that
remain rigid are uprooted, destroyed.
Look also at the captain who hauls his sails too close, who
will not slacken them in the wind, see how he completes his
voyage, keel to the sky.
No, father, yield – give up this passion; allow yourself to
change.
I am young, but if I may be allowed to offer my judgement, I
would say that although men ought to be completely wise by
nature, this is unlikely to be the case and then it is good to
learn from other people's words.

CHORUS: Lord, it would be fair for you to learn from what he's
said. And him from you. You have both spoken well.

KREON: You expect me, at my age, to learn from someone his
age?

HAIMON: Only in what is right.
Don't consider my age but my actions.

KREON: You mean the action of revering those who bring
disorder?

HAIMON: I would not exhort anyone to revere those who are evil.

KREON: Isn't this woman infected with such a disease?

HAIMON: The mass of Thebans do not say so.

116

KREON: Is the city going to tell me how to rule?

HAIMON: Don't you hear how childishly you speak?

KREON: Am I to rule the city with someone else's judgement?

HAIMON: A city is not there for the sake of one man.

KREON: Isn't the city ruled by the one in power?

HAIMON: You would enjoy ruling over an empty country.

KREON: I believe this man is now the ally of a woman.

HAIMON: If you are a woman, yes. My concern is for you.

KREON: You are the worst of the worst.
Claiming to bring your own father to Justice.

HAIMON: It is your own justice I see failing.

KREON: How can I fail when I respect my own rules?

HAIMON: You are not respecting but trampling on the honours
due to the gods.

KREON: You have a foul character, to hide yourself behind a
woman.

HAIMON: I am not the one who will be found to have yielded to
hateful feelings.

KREON: All of your words are for her sake.

HAIMON: No, for your sake, for mine, and for the sake of the gods
below.

KREON: There is no way you will marry that woman still alive.

HAIMON: She will die, then, and in her death destroy someone
else.

HAIMON: Now you have the recklessness to threaten?

HAIMON: How can I threaten when I only express my judgement?

KREON: Don't talk to me of judgement when you're empty of
sense.

HAIMON: Were you not my father, I would have said that you were
not showing good sense.

KREON: You are the slave of a woman and you can stop your
prating.

HAIMON: Do you want always to speak and never to listen?

KREON: Is that so?
Now, by Olympos, know this: it will go hard with you –
heaping blame on me like this. Reviling me.
Bring out the loathsome thing.

Let her die near the bridegroom, yes, now, in front of his very eyes.

HAIMON: No, she will never die in my presence. And you will never see me again. You can go and find yourself other kin to join you in your madness.

CHORUS: He left, lord, with anger in his heart. At that age a man can feel such pain acutely.

KREON: He can act or feel more acutely than any man alive – but he will not save those two girls from their fate.

CHORUS: Are you thinking of killing both of them?

KREON: Not the one who had nothing to do with it. Concerning that matter, you've spoken well.

CHORUS: What kind of fate do you decree for the other?

KREON: I will take her to a desolate path. There I will bury her in a rocky cave – with enough food offered as an expiation – that the city may avoid any pollution.

There she can pray to Death, the only god she honours, and perhaps that will save her life.

Or else she will at last understand that to revere Death is a labour that yields no reward.

FOURTH CHORUS

Desire
never bested in battle
certainly not deterred by wealth
Desire
keeps vigil on a girl's soft cheek
lingers over the sea
trickles down lairs in the wild.

No armour in immortality
Eros
even less in human
ephemerality
where you are, there is madness.

With you, the just turns unjust; the
mind is wrenched aside. Destruction.
With you, enmity ejects kinship. You
stirred up this battle between this
youth, this man.

Triumph in the wistful eyes of this
most beddable bride.

Desire
curls around the oldest laws.
What does it matter what is or is not
allowed
when
Aphrodite wins all?

FOURTH EPISODE

CHORUS: Now, look:
 it is forbidden, I know, but I cannot hold back my tears.
 See:
 Antigone – making her painful way to that marriage chamber,
 eternal sleep.
ANTIGONE: Look at me,
 citizens of my father's land.
 See:
 come to the end – my last path,
 last look at the light of the sun.
 Never again.

 Death,
 who puts all to sleep,
 death leads me still alive to the shore
 of that languorous river, Acheron.
 No wedding song for me,
 no hum outside the bedroom doors.
 No, no song for me at all.
 I will marry that bitter river Death.
 I will marry Acheron.
CHORUS: Yes, but you're joining the corpses in that abyss covered
 with glory and renown.
 You haven't been wasted by disease, you haven't been
 wounded by enemy swords.
 No, according to your own laws and still alive, you will pass
 into Hades.
 No other mortal has done this.
ANTIGONE: I heard once
 of our Phrygian guest, Niobe,
 the daughter of Tantalos.
 I heard
 of her dismal death.
 How on that volcanic crest,
 she felt stone creep like ivy through her limbs –

taming her into
stillness –
stone.
And men tell
how
under the incessant beating of rains
and snow
she dissolves in her grief,
tears flow from her stony brows,
trickle down the cracked rock of her body.
That is the how the gods are taking me
to bed.

CHORUS: Yes, but she was a goddess, born of gods.
We are mere mortals, born of those who die.
Still, it is good to have it said of one who is mortal that her lot
was equal to one of the gods, not only in life, but in death as
well.

ANTIGONE: *Oimoi.*
Now they laugh at me.
I'm to be reviled.
In the name of the gods of my father, can't you wait until I
am dead? Must it be while I stand here before you!
City, city
and you, its well-born citizens.
Streams of the river Dirke
Thebes: sacred grove,
rich chariot ground,
be my witnesses now. See:
how no friend weeps for me.
See according to which laws I am taken to my rocky prison,
my unexpected tomb.
Ill-fortune on me,
an alien among the living and alien among the dead
no longer alive and yet not dead.

CHORUS: You went to the furthest edge of daring, but your foot
hit the high step of Justice and you tripped, child. You inherit
your father's ordeal.

ANTIGONE: Now you're there.
Bleak thoughts, anxiety.
Triple lamentation for my father.
The immeasurable destiny of the renowned Labdakids.
Ruin:
from a mother's bed: ruin
as she sleeps with her own son
with my father
my ill-fated mother.
What kind of parents are these?
The mind reels.
No prayers for me, no marriage.
I go to them,
alien even there –
That was an unlucky marriage, brother, the one you made to
overrun Thebes –
Your death hooks my life.
CHORUS: Reverent behaviour is to be revered, but the powerful
will not brook the transgression of their power.
You knew your own passion and now it has killed you.
ANTIGONE: No weeping, no friend,
no marriage song.
The road is prepared.
My mind reels –
no more glances
on this light, the hallowed,
quivering face of day . . .
no tears over my fate,
no friend,
mourning,
no.
KREON: Don't you know that if laments and wails could affect the
course of death, people would never stop? Take her away
immediately, and in the enfolding dark of that tomb,
abandon her on her own – as I've ordered –
and then she can see whether she wishes to die or live in her
entombment.

We have no guilt as far she is concerned.
She has deprived herself of the right of residence in the
world.
ANTIGONE: That tomb, my wedding chamber, deep dwelling.
For ever.
I go to meet my own
so many of whom are already there, among the dead.
I am the last and the worst by far because I am to join them
even before my life has come to an end. At least I can hope
that my arrival will be
dear to you, father, most dear to you, mother, and dear to
you, my brother.
They were my own hands that bathed you, wreathed your
dead body and poured libations over your tomb. This,
Polyneikes, is my reward for that deed.
What justice of the gods have I offended? And now what gods
must I look to?
Where are my allies?
I have been charged with irreverence for an act of reverence.
If the gods agree, if this seems good to them, then once I've
suffered my punishment, I'll recognize my failing.
But:
if it is these who have failed,
then let them suffer the same evil they have inflicted on me.
CHORUS: Still the same winds storm through her soul.
KREON: Yes, and her guards will have cause to regret their delay.
ANTIGONE: These words bring me near death.
KREON: Forgo any hope this will not come to pass.
ANTIGONE: Land of Thebes, city of my fathers
and you, the first and oldest gods, they lead me away.
Soon, I shall be no more. Look, leaders of Thebes: look,
last descendant of this kingly house.
See:
what I suffer at the hands of what men because I observed,
revered, the rules of reverence.

FIFTH CHORUS

CHORUS

Endure, my child,
listen:
she also endured,
that vibrant princess, Danaë, when her
father made her exchange the light of
the sun for a tomb made of bronze.
She remained hidden,
yoked to that dark chamber.

And yet, my child,
she was of honourable descent
and she had in her womb the seed of
Zeus – thrust in her by his golden rain.

Some try wealth, some go to war, some
build a wall and some take a black ship
across the rough sea, but no one can
ever escape, my child,
the awesome power of their own fate.

Somewhere on the bleak and windswept
coast of a northern sea,
between the Bosporos
and the Thracian city of Salmydessos,
Ares left his city to watch this tale
unfold:
Phineus had two sons, and a new wife.
She was jealous and
Ares saw
how that angry consort
blinded the boys.
He looked on as
she pounded those eyes, struck them

with the sharp point of her weaving
shuttle.
Ares gazed
at those blank bloody circles crying
out for vengeance. He contemplated
the boys as they sat by the beach.
Wasted away. They cried over their
lamentable pain
and the fate of their mother. How
she was badly married – hardly married at all.
Entombed so soon after.
And yet she was the child of the North
Wind,
she was rocked in a cave by the winds
and the storms
and she could climb steep cliffs with
the fastest of horses.
She traced her family far back,
back to the Erechtheids,
yes, a daughter of the gods,
but the long arm of fate
grabbed her too,
my child,
it did.

FIFTH EPISODE

TEIRESIAS: Lords of Thebes, we have shared one road, the two of
us. There is no journey for the blind without a guide.

KREON: What is it, Teiresias, what new?

TEIRESIAS: I shall teach you; listen to the prophet.

KREON: I have never ignored your judgement.

TEIRESIAS: That is why you have steered the city on a straight
course.

KREON: I bear witness to the benefits of your assistance.

TEIRESIAS: Know then that you are once again on the cutting
edge of chance.

KREON: What is it? Your words make me shiver.

TEIRESIAS: Listen and understand the signs that come through
my skill.
I was sitting on the seat from which I observe the birds.
I heard a sound, never heard before, an evil sound.
Birds screeching:
a frenzied cry, barbaric.
I knew they were tearing at each other with bloodied claws –
murderous –
I knew the significance of this whirring of wings.
And immediately, in fear, I placed offerings on the altars.
The fire god refused to set these offerings alight.
Instead,
dank juices oozed from the meat on to the ashes.
Smoke, the fat spits, hisses,
the bile explodes and is scattered in the wind
as the fat which had wrapped the meats away and drips off the
bare bones.
I learned this from the boy who guides me as I guide others –
how the oracles were themselves melting away in obdurate
silence.
Now listen:
Your judgement has made the city ill.
Our altars, our hearths, are cloyed with the foodscraps of
birds and dog-meat, scraps from the dead son of Oedipus –

The gods can no longer receive our prayers, or the fire from the burning of meats.
The birds no longer utter auspicious cries because they are gorged with the bloody fat of the slain man.
And so, my child, consider:
Failure is common to all men. However, a man stops being a fool and unhappy, if, once he has fallen into evil, he moves fast and cures himself.
Stubbornness can sometimes be called ineptitude.
Yield now to the dead man:
no need to goad him further.
What feat of courage is there in killing the dead?
I speak with sound judgement.
It is sweet to learn from someone who speaks well. Especially if he speaks for your benefit.

KREON: Old man:
everyone takes aim at me. Now I'm even to be beset by the tribe of diviners. I am being treated like a pack of merchandise. Bought, then sold. You can trade all the silver of Sardis and all the gold of India, but you will not bury that man in a grave.
Not even if the eagles of Zeus decide to carry the meat to his own throne. Not even the fear of that pollution would make me let you bury the body –
and I know very well that no mortal has the power to defile the gods.
They fall, old man Teiresias, with an ugly fall, those men who, for the sake of gain, try to make ugly words seem beautiful.

TEIRESIAS: *Feu.*
Is there a man here who sees, who thinks –
KREON: What? What common truth will you reveal to us now?
TEIRESIAS: That good advice is the most potent of gifts.
KREON: Yes, and bad judgement can cause great damage.
TEIRESIAS: You are the one riddled with this disease.
KREON: I will not answer a prophet with insults.
TEIRESIAS: You already have, by saying I utter false prophecies.

KREON: The race of prophets loves silver.

TEIRESIAS: And the race of tyrants loves shameful gain.

KREON: Do you know that you are speaking of your ruler?

TEIRESIAS: I know it was through me you saved the city.

KREON: You are a wise prophet, but you love doing wrong.

TEIRESIAS: You will make me say things I want to leave untouched.

KREON: Let them out, but don't speak for the sake of gain.

TEIRESIAS: It will not be for your gain, no.

KREON: My judgement is not for sale. Know that much.

TEIRESIAS: Know this:

The sun will have not have completed many revolutions before you yourself will have given from your own loins a corpse for a corpse –

You will pay heavily for making one who belongs above go down to those below. Yes, you have dishonourably placed a human life in the darkness of a grave.

And you have withheld a death from the gods below – without due share of funeral rites – an object of horror.

This is not your province, nor that of the gods above, whom you've forced in this matter.

Because of this, the anger of Hades treads slowly towards you, and the furies of the gods lie in ambush – to trap you in the same evils.

Consider these things and ask yourself if I needed to be bribed to say them.

Not much time will have passed before the lamentations of men and women rise from your house.

Already there is a tumult of hatred in the countries whose warriors have been licked clean by dogs or wild beasts. Or else, the birds have brought back this putrefaction into the very hearths of the cities.

Grieve now.

These are the arrows I let fly towards you from the passion in my heart. I am a good archer, you will not slip through the heat of my arrows.

Child, take me back to my house.

Let this man loose his passion on younger men.
Let him learn to quiet his tongue and to show greater
intelligence than he has revealed by his present judgements.

CHORUS: He has prophesied terrible things. Since my hair went
grey, I learned this much: he has never told the city a lie.

KREON: To give way is terrible, but to oppose him out of anger
could lead me into ruin even more terrible.

CHORUS: You must heed good advice, Kreon, child of
Menoikeus.

KREON: What must I do? Speak. I'll listen.

CHORUS: Set free the girl embedded in the rock. Bury the exposed
corpse in a grave.

KREON: That's your advice? You think I should yield?

CHORUS: Yes, lord, and quickly. For the avenging gods are swift
of foot and cut down those with bad judgement.

KREON: It goes hard, but I will yield the resolve in my heart. Why
fight an unholy battle with Necessity?

CHORUS: Do these things yourself, don't leave it to others. Do it
now.

KREON: I'll go as I am. Take axes and set out for the place – you
can see it from here –
Since I am the one who imprisoned her, I shall be the one to
set her free.

SIXTH CHORUS

You with the many names,
pride of your nymph mother
Semele,
son of our Thunder God Zeus,
you
guard the glorious stretches of Italy.
Regent of
communal hallows in Eleusis
and of Thebes,
where the Bakchai dance
and the Ismenos flows,
and where the ancestral teeth of the
dragon
were sown,
come, come to us now.
BAKCHOS.

A flash flame casts your shadow
up there on the high crests.
A band of nymphs by the streams of
Kastalia
glitters with you in the water.
A rustle of ivy on the hills of Nysaia.
An abundance of grapes down by the
shore.
The echo of a footfall, the hum of
euion
as you enter the streets of Thebes.
You honour Thebes above all cities,
you and your thunder-stricken mother.
See,
the city snared in a violent plague
Come to us now

with your
purifying tread,
come down from the heights of
Parnassos,
come across the whirring straits.
Come.

Stars exhale their light as you
lead them in the dance.
Choruses fill the night
to your beat. Come,
son of Zeus,
come with your frenzied Thyads,
come dance through the night,
come, generous guide – bearer of gifts –
come to us.
IAKCHOS.

SIXTH EPISODE

MESSENGER: Listen to me, you who live near the palace.
No life stays the same long enough for me to say either that I
approve of it or that I find fault with it.
Chance tips the scales.
Fortune, misfortune, where is the prophet who can predict
how long either will last?
Kreon was to be envied, it seemed to me, once.
He saved this land from its enemies and he had sole rule of
the whole of this country.
Now it cracks and crumbles away.
When a man loses all that gave him joy I say that man is no
longer alive. He's no more than a living corpse. Go on, gorge
yourself with riches, live the life of tyrants, but I wouldn't give
the shadow of smoke to any man for any of these things if
there is no joy.

CHORUS: What is this sorrow of kings you bring with you?

MESSENGER: They are dead. And the living are guilty of their
death.

CHORUS: Who killed? Who's the victim? Speak.

MESSENGER: Haimon is dead. Killed by a kindred hand.

CHORUS: Whose? His father's? His own?

MESSENGER: Himself by himself. But furious with his father – for
that other death.

CHORUS: Oh prophet, your words hit their mark.

MESSENGER: These things are so; now consider the rest.

CHORUS: Here is the unhappy wife of Kreon, Eurydike. Coming
out of the palace. Has she heard? Does she come by chance?

EURYDIKE: Citizens, I heard something as I left the house to
address prayers to the goddess Pallas. I was pulling back the
bolt and opening the doors when I heard whispers of an evil
concerning my house. Full of fear, I leaned against my
servants, fainted.
Repeat the story now. I will listen as someone who is not
unused to evils.

MESSENGER: It is I, dear lady, who can tell you everything.

I was there.

I followed your husband on foot to the outer plain where the body of Polyneikes lay, pitilessly torn apart by the dogs.

He prayed to the goddess of the wayside, Hecate, and then to Pluto, to show him favour and hold back their anger.

He washed the body with pure water, and, heaping young twigs, we burned what was left of it. Then we raised a mound of the dead man's native earth, piled it high.

We walked towards the stony bridal chamber of the girl, bride of Death, as she was now.

One of us had already heard a distant voice, a high wail, coming from that unholy bridal chamber – and came back to tell Kreon of it –

Kreon goes near and is greeted by unintelligible cries.

He groans – says:

Destruction . . .

am I a prophet?

Have I been creeping, unsuspecting, along the most sorrowful road of all?

My child's voice –

Servants, go quickly to the tomb, find the opening and make your way into the cave that I may know whether it was Haimon's voice which leapt at me or the gods deceiving me.

We did as our despondent master bid.

And in the recesses of the tomb we saw her:

hanging from a coil of finely woven linen.

He was prostrate before her, clasping her waist, bewailing this bed of death, his father's deeds and his own star-crossed marriage.

When his father saw the boy, he rushed in with a fearful cry:

Unhappy child, what are you doing there? What are you thinking of? Have you lost your mind? Come out, child, I implore you.

The boy's eyes dart madly. He spits in his father's face.

Then, without a word, he draws his sword. He only just misses his father – who flees.

The ill-fated child now turns his anger on himself. He leans

against the sword and drives it deep into his side. With his
last strength, he holds the girl in a tender embrace.
A jet of blood hits her blanched cheeks.
Corpse embraces corpse.
Sad wedding feast to the music of death,
showing all that an ill-judged act is the greatest evil that can
cling to a man.

CHORUS: What would you make of this?
The woman has turned back, without a word, good or bad.

MESSENGER: I wonder myself. I hope that on hearing about her
child's sufferings, she chose not to lament in front of the
whole city, but went into her own house, with her servants,
there to bewail her private pain.
She is not without judgement or experience; she would not
fail now.

CHORUS: I don't know. Too much silence, too much crying: both
weigh heavily.

MESSENGER: We will know what passions she may have repressed
when we go into the palace, but you speak well. This silence
weighs heavy.

CHORUS: And now your lord comes near, holding in his arms the
woeful evidence.
We can say that this was not a case of ruin at the hands of
another, but of his own failure.

KREON: *Eeoh.*
Failure of a mind that judged so ill.
Stubborn. Deadly.
The killer and the killed.
Look: kinsmen,
woe to my decision.
Eeoh.
Child.
So young; your life – new
Aiai, aiai.
Undone; dead.
The twist of my decision. Not yours.

CHORUS: You see justice now, but it is too late.

134

KREON: *Oimoi.*
    I have learned, yes. Misery.
    A god came crashing down
    and cast me on a wild road.
    Trampled all joy underfoot –
    Feu, feu.
    The pain, the terrible pain of living.
MESSENGER: Master:
    You hold this woe in your arms, but you have more in store
    for you from inside your own house.
KREON: What greater evils can there be than these?
MESSENGER: Your wife is dead. The true mother of this unhappy
    corpse – sharp blows, just now.
KREON: *Eeoh.*
    Hades is still not replete?
    This wasn't sufficient atonement?
    Why this, why such destruction?
    You, making me the butt of evil tidings,
    what did you say?
    Aiai.
    I was dead and you kill me again.
    What did you say? What now? What
    new?
    Aiai.
    Slaughter clasps destruction –
    now a wife's fate.
MESSENGER: You can see yourself.
    (EURYDIKE's *body is brought out.*)
KREON: *Oimoi.*
    Now – this second misery.
    What now? What destiny still gapes for me?
    I've only just held my own son.
    Now, look – another body.
    Feu, feu.
    Piteous mother. Oh, child . . .
MESSENGER: She stood at the altar, raised the sacrificial knife.
    Her eyes clouded.

She lamented that earlier death: her son Megaros.
Then she cried out for this one.
And at last, incantation of evil on you, the childslayer.
KREON: *Aiai.*
Terror –
Will no one plunge a sword – here?
I am at the end of misery.
At the end –
Woe blends with woe.
MESSENGER: She charged you with both fates as she died.
KREON: How did she bring her life to this end?
MESSENGER: She struck herself, here, under the liver, with her own hand, amidst the laments for her child.
KREON: *Oimoi moi.*
Guilt which could hang on no other man.
I, yes, it was I, I killed you, I,
useless –
That is the truth.
And now, citizens, take me away, take me quickly.
I who am nothing, now, no more.
CHORUS: That is the best counsel, if there is any best in evil. It is good to act quickly when such ills lie at our feet.
KREON: Come,
come, supreme fate – a comely fate if this day is my last.
Come, come,
let me not look upon another day.
CHORUS: That is for the future. We must look to what is before us.
KREON: All my desire
in that prayer.
CHORUS: No more prayers. The suffering allotted to mortals cannot be escaped.
KREON: Someone take this senseless man away,
who killed you – child – not willingly
and this woman here.
I'm at the end.
I don't know where to look,

where to lean.
Everything I touch
cracks in my hands.
A grim destiny stalked me –
and sprang.

CHORUS: This is certain: only good judgement secures good
fortune. One must never be irreverent to the gods.
Those who puffed themselves up with great words have been
dealt great blows.
In old age,
they have learned judgement.

FABER DRAMA

W. H AUDEN
ALAN AYCKBOURN
PETER BARNES
SAMUEL BECKETT
ALAN BENNETT
STEVEN BERKOFF
ALAN BLEASDALE
ANNE DEVLIN
T. S ELIOT
BRIAN FRIEL
ATHOL FUGARD
TREVOR GRIFFITHS
CHRISTOPHER HAMPTON
DAVID HARE
TONY HARRISON
VACLAV HAVEL
SHARMAN MACDONALD
FRANK MCGUINNESS
RICHARD NELSON
JOHN OSBORNE
HAROLD PINTER
DENNIS POTTER
SAM SHEPARD
TOM STOPPARD
TIMBERLAKE WERTENBAKER
NIGEL WILLIAMS